Everton

The People's Club

The Giants

The Names

The Match Reports

The Songs

The Managers

The Cult Heroes

The Captains...

...OF THE **CITY'S FIRST** TEAM

'Everton are the people's
club in Liverpool.
The people in the street
support Everton'

- DAVID MOYES
March 2002

Sport Media
A Trinity Mirror Business

WRITTEN BY: DAVID PRENTICE

Produced by Sport Media
Executive Editor: KEN ROGERS Editor: STEVE HANRAHAN
Production Editor: PAUL DOVE Art Editor: RICK COOKE
Research/Production: JAMES CLEARY. Sub Editor: ROY GILFOYLE.
Sales and Marketing Manager: ELIZABETH MORGAN
Designers: BARRY PARKER, COLIN SUMPTER, LEE ASHUN,
GLEN HIND, ALISON GILLILAND, JAMIE DUNMORE, JAMES KENYON
Writers: WILLIAM HUGHES, ALAN JEWELL

Main photographs: Liverpool Daily Post and Echo, Trinity Mirror.
Additional photographs: Action Images
Printed by Scotprint Ltd

FOREWORD BY DAVID MOYES

INTRODUCTION BY 'BEE'
& POWER TO THE PEOPLE

FINAL WORD: BY BILL KENWRIGHT

'It wasn't planned. It just seemed that everyone I met on the street supported Everton. It suits the club perfectly'

I ONLY have one regret about coining the phrase "The People's Club." That is that I didn't patent it first! I must hear that phrase 20 times every day, and it still rings true now as much as it did when I first uttered it in March 2002.

I honestly had no idea quite how much people would relate to it. It has been suggested to me since that I was put up to using the words "People's Club" at my introductory press conference – that some kind of Everton spin doctor suggested it might be a good idea to get the fans onside right from the off.

Nothing could be further from the truth. I never had a conversation with anybody beforehand. What prompted it were my experiences after I knew I had got the job and was preparing to travel to Goodison Park for the press conference.

While I was leaving Preston I kept bumping into people who told me they were Evertonians and wishing me good luck. Everybody I spoke to seemed to be a Blue – and this was in Preston!

Then when I drove into Merseyside everywhere I looked people seemed to be wearing Everton shirts.

It just seemed a natural thing to say – that Everton seemed to be the People's Club of Merseyside.

It wasn't a rehearsed comment. It was just something which came to mind at the time and I didn't attach any significance to it even after I'd said it.

FOREWORD

By the man who invented the famous phrase

Everton

'Everton is not a manufactured club, it's a club that the supporters are born into and bred through. If anything, I think that the phrase has become even more relevant since I said it. It has stuck because the fans have proved it to be accurate'

It was only the next day when I saw all the newspaper headlines that I realised it had struck a chord.

I only wish now that I had patented the phrase before I used it – because it has certainly stuck.

It just felt right at the time.

Everton is not a manufactured club, it's a club that the supporters are born into and bred through. If anything, I think that the phrase has become even more relevant since I said it.

It has stuck because the fans have proved it to be accurate.

Even if we move to a new stadium in Kirkby it will still be accurate, because it describes a state of mind, an attitude rather than a geographical location. It sums up the people rather than the place.

But the "People's Club" is something which will move with the club. It struck a chord with Evertonians, and I have to say it caused a bit of a stir across the park, too.

I'd only been in the Everton job four weeks when a Liverpool fan sent me a photograph which I found really funny.

A message came with it saying: 'Call yourselves the People's Club? You're just the Village People's Club!'

With it there was a picture of the pop group with my face, Duncan Ferguson's, David Unsworth and Kevin Campbell all superimposed over the band.

I thought it was really funny, but it still didn't change my mind ... that Everton is the People's Club of Merseyside.

Mersey rivalry:
Saluting a famous
derby win in 2006

'We are THE people of the football world. This is the first time a Liverpool club had its hands on t'Coop'

DAVID MOYES might have coined the 'People's Club' phrase for the first time in 2002 - but it wasn't the first occasion the Blues had been called a club of the people.

In fact, almost a century before, a local sports reporter who operated under the pseudonym "Bee" kicked off his report of the 1906 FA Cup final with the words: 'WE are THE people of the football world.'

Under the headlines 'OUR CUP – LIVERPOOL CITY TAKE ALL THE HONOURS – HOW EVERTON WON,' Bee gave a colourful account of the great exodus of Evertonians to the capital.

In the Liverpool Daily Post of Monday, April 23, 1906, he wrote: 'We are THE people of the football world. The Liverpool Football Club had taken the first honour a week ago (Liverpool had been crowned league champions); it remained for Everton to complete the delightful double.

'They did as they were expected. This is the first time a Liverpool club has had its hands on t'Coop, and altogether the season's ending is one crammed full of brilliant results.'

Alex 'Sandy' Young's goal 13 minutes from time brought the FA Cup back to Merseyside for the first time, and the match reports of the day ran to several thousand words.

But Bee's account of the big day, Edwardian style, is worth recounting.

Train was the only realistic way for supporters to travel long distances and he reported: 'The Liverpool excursionists must have numbered seven or eight thousand and Newcastle people were not very far behind this number.

'Lime-Street, Birkenhead and other stations presented a most unusual sight at midnight on Friday, and the later trains were packed with excursionists.

'Midnight travelling has its disadvantages when you have an enthusiastic set of companions and, with the varied musical efforts of Mersey merchants and their mouth organs, concertinas and cornets, I should imagine there were some hundreds who were not able to get even forty winks in their long journey.

'On the return journey there was a great change. Trippers had exhausted their lung power and had enthused as much as they possibly could, and though at the stations they had gathered together thousands of bottles of lubrication, they were distinctly orderly and respectable and nine-tenths of the people on the return journey, exhausted after a capital outing, slept the whole journey through.'

The description of the fans' day out for the first successful Cup final doesn't sound too dissimilar to day trips for modern Cup finals!

Of course the venue in 1906 was completely different to the Wembley Stadium which later became synonymous with the FA Cup Final.

Before 1895 a variety of venues had been employed, including Goodison Park in 1894, but from 1895 up until the outbreak of War in 1914, the grand and glorious Crystal Palace became the Cup Final's traditional home.

But even in 1906, the choice of the capital as a Cup final venue was not cause for universal approval.

'Some people rather object to the Crystal Palace company having the final, year after year', added Bee 'but I think they are mostly critics who have not been to the Palace.

First heroes of the city: Jack Sharp was one of the men who brought the FA Cup to Liverpool for the first time

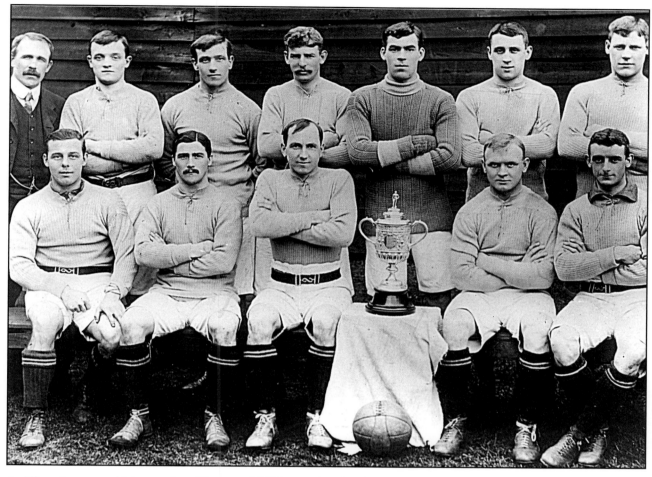

And if you know your history makers: The men of 1906 were already building the reputation of Everton in the city and beyond

'The ground does not allow the League footballer to reproduce his skill on the extreme wing, but it certainly nationalises the game and a tie outside London would not be a final tie.'

Match reports of the Edwardian era are long, detailed and, to 21st century sensibilities, interminally dull.

But the nature of Everton's first Cup success can be gleaned from the following excerpts.

'On arriving at the big glass house we settled ourselves down with umbrella near at hand, because the weather, from opening gloriously fine, broke down and ended in a dull afternoon.

'Just a few spots fell from nature's weather cart, but bless you, this was a Providential rain, being sufficient to lay the dust to the Palace road and insufficient to cause discomfort to one soul of the 75,608 people present within the walls of the Palace.

'One shudders to think how the crowd would have fared had rain been plentiful, for the enclosure has extremely little covered accommodation.

'The turf was hard, hard as nails, and this was a potent factor against football of the quality we know the

competitors to be capable of.

'Add to this there was a breeze which varied its course at almost every minute and you will imagine how awkward it was for the 22-men to gauge the swervings and curvings of the ball.

'The final of 1906 will go down in the records as a poor exhibition which, though accurate, does not do the victors' credit.

'Everton, by pluck, determination and by thinking out their best mode of play, gained a thoroughly earned victory.

'They were masters of the situation, even though Newcastle tried every means of reviving their position.

'Briefly Balmer defended magnificently and with coolness, the halves Taylor, Abbott and Makepeace were in their best form and T'was these three who made the game so tame, while of the forwards Sharp was overworked and crowned his work with that absolutely accurate cross which enabled Young to beat Lawrence.

'We raise our voices loud and long and shout "Hurrah for Everton."'

PEOPLE
PASSION

The fans who make
the club so special

1878

Everton

THE power of the people has been highlighted many times at the People's Club.

The occasions when players have been inspired by the noise from the terraces are legend.

"Just put the ball into the box and the Gwladys Street will suck the ball in," Howard Kendall told his players at half-time during the most famous night in Goodison Park's long history.

The Blues were trailing Bayern Munich 1-0 in the semi-final, second leg of the European Cup Winners' Cup.

Forty-five minutes later they were celebrating a 3-1 win and goalscorer Andy Gray said of the decisive second goal touched in by himself: "Howard was right. The fans must have sucked it in because I didn't hit it very hard!"

That was in April 1985 – at the peak of the greatest run of success the club had ever enjoyed.

Just 15 months earlier, however, with the Blues almost at rock bottom and the manager's position reportedly hinging on an FA Cup tie at Stoke City, the fans proved their worth again.

It became known as the day the fans delivered Howard Kendall's teamtalk.

More than 5,000 had made their way down the M6 to Stoke's Victoria Ground, and after the match Kendall explained: "We could hear our fans from the dressing room before the match and, with due respect, our record has not been so good that they should come down in their thousands like that.

"So we opened the dressing room windows to hear them better. That was better than any team talk I could deliver.

"They were absolutely fantastic.

"They haven't had much to shout about in recent weeks but they turned up in their thousands to urge us on.

"As we sat in the dressing room before the game I opened the window.

"The noise which came in was deafening; it was far more inspirational than any team talk I could have given."

Alan Irvine, a player that afternoon but later to take up the managerial mantle himself as David Moyes' assistant, added: "They were absolutely fantastic and got right behind us from the start.

"We could hear them singing before the game and they went on to completely outshine the home fans.

"It makes a difference when you have that level of backing."

It made a difference that afternoon.

Everton won the match 2-0 thanks to goals from Andy

Gray and Alan Irvine, and *Echo* reporter Nick Hilton was under no illusions as to what made the difference.

'The 5,000 Evertonians who sang, shouted and supported their team as if they were already the FA Cup winners celebrated joyously at the end.

'Full-back John Bailey led the Everton players in applause of appreciation to the blue hordes – and rightly so.

'For this was one of those occasions when supporters played a significant role in lifting their team to victory.'

They were prophetic words.

Four months later those same Everton fans were celebrating the club's first silverware for 14 years as Kevin Ratcliffe raised the FA Cup at Wembley Stadium.

Seven years earlier the famous old arena had reverberated to the sounds of Mersey voices once again, this time in the club's first appearance in a League Cup final.

The 1977 final against Aston Villa ended goalless, necessitating a replay at Hillsborough.

And once again the power of the people was evident, as Charles Lambert's commentary in the following night's *Echo* underlined.

'The League Cup final, this incredible story of sweat and effort and some of the most committed tackling ever seen, is the vehicle through which Everton are forming a communion with their supporters,' he reported.

'So many times in the past Goodison Park has worn an air of detachment, with the spectators looking on politely like ancients watching the youngsters at play.

'Goodison would hardly have recognised the scenes at Hillsborough last night, just as it would not have recognised those at Wembley on Saturday.

'There is a new spirit on the terraces – and in the stands, too, for last night the chant of "Everton are magic," a chant which looks like becoming their new theme song, came from the stands as much as from the other parts of the ground.

'It is a spirit which is not easily related to the days not so very long ago when Goodison echoed not to hymns of adulation, but to the thuds of cushions landing on the turf.

'The point is, Everton have still not won anything. The fans are not waiting for success before making themselves heard; they are weighing in with their contribution in a bid to achieve that success.

'Last night proved it. They outshouted the Villa clans from before the start, but did they pack up when they went a goal down?

'Did they sidle away when the last seconds were running out?

'Did they hell! They kept up the chorus of "Everton are Magic!" and Bob Latchford proved they were right.'

It just goes to show one thing: You should never under-estimate the power of the people at the People's Club!

Grand old support: Backing the Blues in Rotterdam and (opposite) Wembley

'The point is, Everton have still not won anything. The fans are not waiting for success before making themselves heard; they are weighing in with their contribution to achieve that success. Last night proved it'

People's Club The Giants

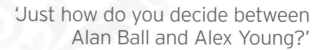

'Just how do you decide between
Alan Ball and Alex Young?'

THEY are the pillars of the People's Club – the individuals officially recognised as having had the greatest impact in the development of Everton Football Club.

As a result they have been granted the status of Millennium Giants, and placed on an elite pedestal at Goodison Park. In the weeks before the turn of the new millennium, Everton decided to install 10 individuals as the greatest in the club's history – one for every decade of the 20th century.

But just how do you decide between Alan Ball and Alex Young? How can you choose one Everton great from 1980s icons like Neville Southall, Kevin Ratcliffe, Peter Reid, Graeme Sharp and Andy Gray? And where do players whose careers spanned two decades – Dixie Dean in the 1920s and 1930s, Ted Sagar in the 1930s and 1940s and Neville Southall in the 1980s and 1990s – fit in?

They were just some of the challenges thrown down to the 10-man panel. The make-up of the panel itself was a painstaking process.

All 10 individuals were steeped in the history and heritage of Everton. Club officials wanted to ensure they had a cross-section of as many diverse and informed views as possible before selecting such a prestigious Hall of Fame. The panel members certainly fitted that bill.

Then chairman Sir Philip Carter presided over the most successful period of trophy gathering in the club's history, had been a director of the club for more than 20

CHAPTER 1

The Millennium Giants, who form the foundation of the People's Club

'Their conversations were lively, sometimes heated, but always entertaining. The exercise proved so popular – and there were so many legendary figures who didn't make the original top 10, that it was decided to elect a new face every year'

years – and a supporter even longer. Now he is honorary life president.

Bill Kenwright was deputy chairman in the autumn of 1999, while of course now he is even more active than ever as chairman of the club. Howard Kendall once famously described his relationship with the club as "a marriage." And he offered a unique insight from two very different perspectives of some of the players under consideration. He was a team-mate of sixties and seventies stars like Alan Ball, Brian Labone, Colin Harvey and Joe Royle – then he managed the all-conquering class of the 1980s.

Brian Labone offered informed insight into the earlier half of the 1960s, while Graeme Sharp's Everton career encompassed all of the ecstatic eighties. Dave Hickson was the expert on the 1950s, while a view from the other side of the pitch hoardings came from then *Liverpool Echo* sports editor Ken Rogers and his Everton correspondent David Prentice. The fans were represented by leading figures from two supporters' clubs, Jim King of the Everton (Goodison) Supporters' Club and Ian MacDonald of the Everton Independent Supporters' Club.

The panel met for two brain-storming sessions – appropriately enough in the Goodison Park boardroom. Their conversations were lively, sometimes heated, but always entertaining. The exercise proved so popular – and there were so many legendary figures who didn't make the original top 10, that it was decided to elect a new face every year. Their names and stories follow later.

So here are the pillars of the People's Club, the select band who form Everton's Millennium Giants.

Panel members: Dave Hickson, Bill Kenwright and (opposite page, right) the late, great Brian Labone

'All-rounder and Goodison's own 'Pocket Hercules' who made a name for himself'

SHARP was an apt name for a winger of breathtaking brilliance, who combined impeccable sportsmanship with his outstanding talents in two sporting fields.

Each of Everton's 10 Millennium Giants were leading figures in the world of association football. Only one, however, achieved international honours in two sporting arenas!

Jack Sharp was a goalscoring outside-right, whose dashing wing-play and thunderous shooting earned him two international caps for England.

A supremely talented cricketer as well, however, he also won three Test caps for his country – and scored a century against Australia in 1909.

It was his performances over 342 appearances in an Everton jersey, however, which earned him inclusion as our first Millennium Giant of the century.

Signed from Aston Villa in 1899, he was a short, stocky man described by one writer of the day as a 'Pocket Hercules.'

A lightning-fast sprinter, he possessed the ability to flight pinpoint centres onto the head of Everton's marauding centre-forward of the day, Alex "Sandy" Young, or cut inside his full-back to unleash shots of fierce power.

In the days when a sports star's popularity was measured by the number of times his portrait appeared on cigarette cards, Jack Sharp had 14 different cards created for him.

Only two Evertonians could boast more – Dixie Dean, the most celebrated player in the Football League, and Harry Makepeace, who followed Sharp as an England international at football and cricket.

Renowned as much for his sportsmanship and fair play as his wing wizardry, Sharp's career almost perfectly encompassed the first decade of the 20th century.

He made his debut on the opening day of the 1899-1900 campaign – and ended his one-club career on the final day of the 1909-1910 season.

His career had threatened to become a series of near misses – after three runners-up spots in the First Division Championship and an FA Cup final defeat in 1907. But he became a winner on April 21, 1906 – and was

instrumental in helping Everton bring the FA Cup back to Merseyside for the first time.

With the Crystal Palace Cup final against Newcastle United heading for a goalless stalemate, there was an exchange in midfield between Jack Taylor and Jimmy Settle.

The ball was switched out to the feet of Jack Sharp who, according to a contemporary newspaper report 'resisted the attentions of McWilliam and dashing along centred like a flash clean into the goalmouth, where Young, smartly following up after the leather, finished the job in style!

'Needless to say, the pent-up feelings of the multitude broke forth in such a volume of sound that it was a wonder the threatening rain-clouds overhead did not discharge their deluge.'

Sharp's eventual decision to retire, after a decade of stalwart service, was influenced by witnessing the tragic and premature end to a team-mate's career.

Jack Taylor was forced to quit, according to Thomas Keates' *Jubilee History of the Club*, by a 'disabling blow to his larynx' in an FA Cup semi-final against Barnsley. Sharp followed a month later, but his devotion to Everton remained undimmed.

After the decision a club historian, Mr Pickford, commented: "No player's brilliance on the field was more vividly impressed on the minds of the Everton spectators than Jack Sharp's."

He continued to impress himself on the supporters' minds in a new role as club director, a position he held with distinction for many years.

JACK SHARP FACTFILE

Born: Hereford, 1879
Everton Appearances: 342
Everton Goals: 80
Everton Honours: FA Cup winner 1906
FA Cup runner-up 1907
First Division Championship
runner-up 1901-02, 1904-05, 1908-09
England caps: 2
Football League appearances: 3

'... he placed the ball for a corner, then calmly dribbled it through the goalmouth'

SAM Chedgzoy holds a claim to fame few footballers of his, or any other generation, could claim.

He forced a change in the laws of football!

The bizarre and far-reaching incident took place after the FA had reworded the corner-kick rule in their statute book in June 1924.

The drafting of the law left a loophole, spotted by *Liverpool Echo* sports editor Ernest Edwards.

He spoke to officials at Everton about the wording of the clause and Chedgzoy, the Blues' regular corner taker, agreed to expose the limitations of the law.

"There's nothing in the book as it stands to prevent you dribbling the ball right into the middle instead of kicking it from the corner," explained Mr Edwards.

"Why not try it out and see what happens?"

Always willing to enter into the spirit of things, Chedgzoy did just that.

In a match early that season, he placed the ball for a corner-kick, then calmly dribbled it through to the goalmouth, while referee, linesmen and players stood dumbfounded. The referee began to lecture Sam, but primed by Ernest Edwards, the winger innocently declared: "What's in the rules to stop me doing it ref?"

There wasn't anything.

But there was an emergency meeting of the Football League afterwards and the law was altered.

While Chedgzoy became famous for that incident, it did not overshadow the immense contribution he made to Everton Football Club as a dashing right-winger of pace and style.

Like future Blues legend Joe Mercer, Chedgzoy learned his football in the hard school of Ellesmere Port football.

He was first spotted as a 20-year-old, plying his trade down the right flank of the Burnell's Iron Works side in the West Cheshire League. The man who spotted him was Fred Geary, a record-breaking Everton centre-forward of the Victorian era.

Geary had amassed the incredible total of 86 goals in 98 Everton appearances between 1889 and 1895 – and clearly appreciated the service a quality winger could provide.

Chedgzoy became the successor to the great Jack

Sharp, and the greatest compliment that could be paid to him is that he did not suffer in the comparison.

Bobby Parker was the centre-forward who benefited most notably from Chedgzoy's blistering pace, bewitching technique and ability to hang centres in opposition penalty boxes.

In 1914-15 Everton clinched their second League title, with Parker contributing 36 goals in 35 appearances. Many were supplied by the right boot of Chedgzoy.

Ironically, when the young Dixie Dean kicked off his colossal Everton career in 1925-26, Chedgzoy was enjoying his final season in an Everton jersey. Evertonians can only imagine the havoc that pairing would have wreaked on First Division defences!

Despite having four years wiped from his playing record by the First World War, Chedgzoy still went on to amass 300 appearances for the Blues.

It wasn't until his 30th birthday that he was first recognised by his country – in an international against Wales – but he went on to collect eight England caps and also represented the Football League on five occasions.

At the end of his career he left Liverpool for Montreal, where he continued to play until he was 51. He made regular visits back to England, but settled permanently in Canada where he died in 1967, aged 78.

SAM CHEDGZOY FACTFILE

Born: Ellesmere Port, 1890
Everton Appearances: 300
Everton Goals: 36
Everton Honour: First Division
Championship winner 1914-15
England caps: 8
Football League appearances: 5

No.3:   **1920-1929**

'Quick, sharp and intelligent, his greatest quality was undoubtedly his aerial ability'

ARGUABLY the greatest goalscorer ever to grace the English game, undeniably the greatest Everton player of all-time, William Ralph Dean's name was the first installed in the Millennium Giants roster.

His selection provoked the least debate. The only argument concerning a man whose achievements spanned two decades was, in what period?

He scored 164 of his 383 Everton goals in the 1920s (this tally includes six FA Charity Shield strikes, not included in some record books).

In the 1930s he captained the club to an unprecedented treble of Second Division, First Division and FA Cup triumphs. But the achievement for which he is best remembered is the individual goalscoring record of 60 League goals in a single season - a record set in 1928 and never beaten since. For that reason Dean was selected in the decade in which his unparalleled powers first emerged - and peaked.

Signed from Tranmere Rovers for £3,000 in 1925, he scored 32 League goals in his first full season as an Evertonian.

'His ability to play football ever again was questioned, following a motorcycle accident in which his skull and jaw were fractured'

That was just six goals short of the then League record of 38, held by another former Everton centre-forward, Bert Freeman.

But his chances of eventually overtaking the record were severely doubted during the summer of 1926. Indeed, his ability to play football ever again was questioned, following a motorcycle accident in which his skull and jaw were fractured.

Thomas Keates' *Jubilee History of Everton Football Club* recorded: 'Doctors were afraid he could not live for many hours.

'His survival astonished them. When recovery was assured the medical pronouncement was: "This man will never be able to play football again."'

Play again he did, to such startling effect that romantic tales began to surround his spell in hospital.

Quick, sharp and intelligent in his centre-forward play, his greatest quality was undoubtedly his astonishing aerial ability.

'Ordinary players butt the ball with the crown of their heads,' wrote a contemporary report. 'Dean artistically glides it downwards with the side of his head. In this respect he excels every other famous centre-forward.'

Such was his success that envious contemporaries began to suggest that surgeons had left a steel plate in his skull following his life-saving surgery.

The stories, of course, were nonsensical, but indicate the aura which surrounded the man.

His record-breaking season of 1927-28, when Everton claimed the League Championship, was a *Roy of the Rovers*-style saga.

Dean scored in each of the first nine matches of the season - including all five in a 5-2 home defeat of Manchester United.

By Christmas he was halfway to his target. Goals 41, 42 and 43 came at Anfield in a 3-3 draw, but then a four-game drought when nobody in an Everton jersey scored seemed to put the brakes on the record-charge.

With nine matches remaining, Dean needed 17 goals for the record - a seemingly impossible target.

But after doubles against Derby County, Blackburn Rovers, Sheffield United and Aston Villa were netted, a sparkling four-goal haul at Burnley put the record in sight again.

Worryingly, Dean had to leave the Turf Moor pitch through injury and he was nursed diligently through the next seven days by trainer Harry Cook.

He was eventually declared fit for the final match of the season, at home to Herbert Chapman's legendary Arsenal side, but needed a hat-trick for the record.

The Gunners had the famous Charles Buchan playing his final match before retirement in their defence, eager to ensure Everton's young upstart didn't steal HIS show.

It was, however, undeniably Dean's day.

A header and a penalty-kick equalled George Camsell's record, then with time ticking away Dean broke the

record outright.

'Five minutes from time we made up our minds that Dixie wasn't going to get the other goal we longed to see,' wrote Thomas Keates.

'Good heavens! While the thought was formulating, Troup (the electric tripper) sent a nice dropping shot in front of goal, the ball hung in the air, Dixie's magical head went for it and tipped it into the net.

'You talk about explosions, and loud applause; we have heard many explosions, and much applause in our long pilgrimage. But, believe us, we have never heard such a prolonged roar of thundering, congratulatory applause before as to that which ascended to heaven when Dixie broke the record.'

This was only the first significant achievement of Dean's long and successful playing career - but it is still the most memorable.

Everton were relegated for a single season in 1930-31, but Second Division defences were no match for a striker of Dean's talents. During the promotion campaign he scored more goals than matches he actually played in!

He captained Everton to a further title success in 1932, scoring another astonishing 45 League goals in 38 games, then in 1933 he led Everton to FA Cup glory at Wembley.

Typically, he scored in every round except the semi-final - and with shirt numbering introduced for the first time at Wembley to aid radio listeners, became the first Everton No. 9.

He continued to score regularly throughout his career.

Revered for his sportsmanship as well as his burgeoning talent, he was never once booked or dismissed - despite the kind of provocation which once saw him lose a testicle in a match.

For a man whose life was linked so indelibly with Everton Football Club, it was fitting that he died at Goodison Park in March 1980, minutes after the final whistle of a derby match.

'DIXIE' DEAN FACTFILE

Born: Birkenhead 1907
Everton Appearances: 433
Everton Goals: 383
Everton Honours: First Division Championship winner 1927-28, 1931-32
Second Division Championship winner 1930-31
FA Cup Winner 1933
FA Charity Shield winner 1928, 1932
England caps: 16
Football League appearances: 6

'I tried to make collecting crosses my life's work. I would practice for hours on end'

THE duration of Ted Sagar's Everton career eventually became the main reason for his fame.

He spent 24 years and one month in an Everton No. 1 jersey - and held the club's appearance record until another member of the Goodison goalkeeping union surpassed his 463 League game target.

But it wasn't just endurance which saw him overhaul thirties legends like Tommy Lawton and Joe Mercer in our Millennium Giants search. Sagar was an enduring footballer. But he was also an outstanding one.

'There is no finer goalkeeper in the League today,' opined one newspaper, on the occasion he was selected to represent the Football League in 1934.

That came five years after he joined Everton from the humble origins of Thorne Colliery FC in Yorkshire. That was March, 1929 - and on January 18, 1930 he made the first of what was to become a record-breaking 463 League appearances, against Derby County.

Little realising the career which was about to unfold, the *Liverpool Echo* recorded: 'This will be Sagar's first turn for the senior side, and as he has accomplished some good work in the Central League, it is expected that the test will not be too much for him.'

It wasn't. Everton won 4-0, and Sagar enjoyed eight more run-outs that season.

Slim and underweight for a goalkeeper, in the days when it was legitimate for tough, tall centre-forwards to bounce both goalkeeper and ball into the net, Sagar survived by sheer skill. He had an uncanny ability to judge the high flight of a ball from the flanks, and he was completely unafraid. Ahead of his time, he tried to perfect the art of collecting crosses.

"I tried to make collecting crosses my life's work," he explained in a contemporary interview.

"I would practice for hours on end, week in week out, with a couple of lads pushing high balls into the box and another one coming in to tackle me as I grabbed. Eventually I could do it by instinct and once I got hold of the ball, I very seldom got it knocked out of my hands."

Sagar's debut season saw Everton endure the ignominy of relegation from the top flight for the first time. Left out of the promotion campaign the very next year, he was recalled for the following momentous season - a League title charge.

After his first full season ended with a League Championship medal in his pocket, in 1933 he added an FA Cup winner's medal to his collection - when he kept a clean sheet at Wembley against Manchester City.

In 1938-39 he became a League champion again - and only the outbreak of War prevented him adding to that haul. War-time, however, did allow him to add one unique entry to his playing log. Capped four times by England, he also gained the distinction of playing for Northern Ireland during the War. Stationed in Portadown with the Signal Corps, Northern Ireland were short of a goalkeeper for a War-time international against Southern Ireland when they turned to Sagar.

He was delighted to accept the invitation - and was proud of his achievement at representing two countries at international level. He often described his most pleasurable match as a footballer, however, as a derby game at Goodison in September 1934.

"A late Dixie Dean goal won us the game," he later recalled. "I think it was one of the greatest games I ever played. Liverpool seemed to hit me that day with everything but the stand - and I managed to keep them out. It is a wonderful feeling to beat the local rivals. I wouldn't say it is the most important match of the season on your own ground - but it is one of them."

Sagar's last appearance came at Goodison against Tranmere in May 1953, in the Liverpool Senior Cup final. After his retirement he served as landlord of the Blue Anchor in Aintree, where nothing pleased him more than regaling the regulars with stories of his playing days.

He died in 1986, aged 76, and at his funeral another Everton legend, the great Joe Mercer, declared: "He was a spectacular player who was truly out on his own. I can't compare him with any of today's players - I can only describe him as an original, a one-off."

TED SAGAR FACTFILE

Born: Moorends, Yorkshire, 1910
Everton Appearances: 499
Everton Goals: 0
Everton Honours: First Division Championship winner 1931-32, 1938-39
FA Cup winner 1933
FA Charity Shield winner 1932
England caps: 4
Football League appearances: 5

'There were games when I went on and didn't break sweat. It was that good'

THE words Thomas George Jones mean little to most Evertonians.

But mention the name T.G. Jones, as the man was more commonly known, and supporters of a certain vintage instantly conjure up images of one of the coolest, classiest and most unruffled of central defenders ever to pull on the Royal Blue jersey.

Regarded as one of the footballing scientists of his day, Everton decided to invest £3,000 in his talents after just six League matches for Wrexham.

One of his team-mates, Gordon Watson, was in no doubt it was one of the shrewdest pieces of transfer business the club ever conducted.

"T. G. Jones was the best signing that Everton ever made," he declared. "When the opposition got a corner-kick, he used to head the ball back to the goalkeeper, Ted Sagar.

"Nine times out of 10 Ted would play holy hell with you if you passed the ball back to him. He used to say 'I've got enough to do watching these fellows, as well as passing back from our own players.' But never with T.G."

He won a League Championship medal in only his second full season with the Blues, but a truly outstanding Everton team was prevented from adding to that honour by the Second World War.

"We won the League by Easter," recalled T.G. "We were a great side. They called us 'The School of Science.' Believe me when I tell you there were games I went on the field and didn't break sweat. It was that good."

The War wiped out five full seasons from his first-class record, but when hostilities ceased in 1946, the break had done little to tarnish Jones' style.

Indeed, in 1947 Italian giants Roma made prolonged attempts to lure him to the eternal city in the days when transfers between European clubs were rare.

Everton reluctantly accepted a bid of £15,000, and were as relieved as Roma were disappointed when the deal fell through because of foreign exchange issues.

Jones continued to exhibit his individual brand of calm assurance at the heart of Everton's defence, and he was appointed club captain in 1949 in succession to Peter Farrell.

No.5:   1940-1949

Both opponents and supporters alike were convinced the honour was long overdue.

Jim King, Secretary of the Everton Supporters' (Goodison) Club and a member of the Millennium Giants panel, said: "He was known as the 'Prince of Centre-halves.'

"He was absolutely brilliant, cool under pressure, good in the air and brilliant on the ground. What always stands out in my opinion of T.G., if he took a free-kick, say from the edge of his own box, he'd just stroll up, no effort at all, perfectly positioned, correct-kicking and all that, and the ball would zoom into the other penalty area. The man was absolute perfection."

Former Liverpool star of the same era, Cyril Done, added: "T. G. was a gentleman off the field, and a gentleman on the field.

"I think he was the only player I ever knew who could dribble a ball on his own six-yard line and come out with it still between his feet.

"He was a brilliant footballer. I jumped up to head a ball with him once, and he came down, fell awkwardly and hurt his ankle very badly. I'm not sure if he broke it.

"A lot of people seemed to think that I had injured him. I was very upset at the very idea that I could be considered as injuring the great T. G. Jones."

After a 14-year Everton career packed full of memories, T. G. hung up his boots. One of his most precious memories, however, was an unusual one.

"There are not many people about now who can say they played alongside Dixie Dean," he said from his newsagents office in North Wales.

T. G. Jones now ranks alongside his hero as one of Everton's Millennium Giants.

T.G. JONES FACTFILE

Born: Connahs Quay, 1917
Everton Appearances: 178
Everton Goals: 5
Everton Honour: First Division Championship winner 1938-39
Wales caps: 17
War-time internationals: 11

'A swashbuckling centre-forward ready to give blood for the Royal Blue cause'

No.6:   1950-1959

THE 1950s was the decade which unleashed rock 'n' roll on an unsuspecting world.

With his towering blond quiff, rumbustious playing style and engaging personality, Dave Hickson was Everton's very own equivalent of a rock 'n' roll star.

A swashbuckling centre-forward ready to give blood for the Royal Blue cause - which he did, frequently - he grabbed the affection and imagination of the Everton supporters like few other players have, before or since.

The 1950s were a lacklustre period for Everton Football Club, but Hickson constantly provided a charismatic cocktail of goals, unswerving commitment and occasional scrapes with opponents and officials.

He had the finest possible mentor as a young player - the incomparable Dixie Dean - who coached him when he played for Cheshire Army Cadets.

His raw potential soon became obvious and, like so many famous Blues before him, the young striker was discovered by Blues' boss Cliff Britton playing non-League football in Ellesmere Port.

He was taken to Everton in 1948, but had his career put on temporary hold by the call of National Service.

He was first called to the Royal Blue colours in September 1951 at Leeds United - incidentally, the last time Everton won a League match at Elland Road until the hoodoo was broken in 2002 - and soon cemented a permanent place in the first team. In 1953, he established his place in Everton folklore.

The Blues were enduring one of only four seasons outside the top division in 1952-53, when they embarked upon a stirring FA Cup run.

After home wins over Ipswich Town and Nottingham Forest, mighty Manchester United were drawn to visit Goodison Park in the fifth round.

Predictably the visitors took the lead, before Tommy Eglington snatched an equaliser - and Hickson made his bid for Everton immortality.

In the days before substitutes were allowed, Hickson typically threw his blond quiff in amongst flying boots and emerged with a wicked gash over his eyebrow.

He left the pitch to have the injury stitched - and 10 team-mates and 50,000 supporters gloomily accepted that Everton would be a man down for the remainder of the match.

They reckoned without Hickson's unfailing courage.

An ear-splitting roar greeted his return to the fray - with five stitches hastily inserted in the wound - and minutes later he scored the match-winner.

As if to confirm his warrior's stature, he re-opened the wound in a heading duel, resisted pleas by team-mates and referee to leave the field again, and eventually retired after 90 minutes to a hero's ovation.

He scored a spectacular match-winner in the quarter-final, too, against Aston Villa - before the Blues' brave bid for Wembley glory ended in a seven-goal thriller in Manchester against Bolton Wanderers.

A star had been born during that rousing run, however, and the following season Hickson hammered 25 League goals in the successful promotion campaign.

After one season back in the top flight, Cliff Britton sold Hickson to Aston Villa, but the player could never settle away from Goodison.

A spell at Huddersfield Town was similarly short-lived and he returned to his spiritual home in August 1957.

The goals weren't quite as free-flowing second time around - but there was still a riotous outcry when he was allowed to leave Everton again two years later.

The problem was his next port of call - Liverpool Football Club!

The deal sparked outrage amongst Everton and Liverpool supporters alike - until he scored on his Anfield debut to silence one section of the doubters.

He later went on to play for Tranmere Rovers - and while it is one of Dave Hickson's many claims to fame that he is one of the few professional footballers ever to have played for all three Merseyside clubs, there has never been any doubt as to where his heart lies.

Still employed by the club as a guide on the popular Stadium Tours, he remains an Everton man and to this day shows people proudly around the ground he graced so loyally throughout the 1950s.

DAVE HICKSON FACTFILE

Born: Salford, 1929
Everton Appearances: 243
Everton Goals: 111
Everton Honour: Division Two runner-up 1953-54

'Brian Labone was once booed by the home crowd because he injured Young'

ALEX YOUNG or Alan Ball?

The inspirational firebrand who combined passion and polish, or the sublime artist who was almost deified by the fans?

The panel's choice as to who should be the Millennium Giant for the 1960s provoked the most heated discussion of all.

Men who shared the same pitch as Alan Ball were adamant he deserved the accolade. Those who observed the matchless grace of "The Golden Vision" were equally insistent about the claims of their hero.

In the end there was the Millennium Giants equivalent of a voting recount - with the almost venerated Scotsman winning the day.

During his playing peak Alex Young inspired equally passionate emotions.

His hero worship on one half of Merseyside during the "Swinging Sixties" bordered on the hysterical.

When Harry Catterick left Young on the sidelines to blood a promising centre-forward named Joe Royle in 1966, the Everton manager was jostled in the Blackpool FC car park by his own supporters.

Brian Labone, no less, was once booed by the home crowd because he had accidentally injured Young in a training session.

So why the fuss?

In sum, Alex Young came possibly as close as any single player to embodying the essence of the *Soccer School of Science*.

He stroked the ball, rather than kicked it.

He glided across even the heaviest of surfaces, shimmying and tricking his way past clogging defenders before effortlessly floating shots past baffled goalkeepers.

A deep-lying centre-forward, he was never in the same mould as traditional Everton No. 9s like Dean, Lawton and Hickson, but he possessed incredible spring and could hang in the air to meet crosses before dispatching bullet headers with one flick of his blond halo.

Signed in November 1960 from Hearts for £40,000, Scottish experts reckoned Young was too inconsistent and too peripheral to cut it in England.

They were proved spectacularly wrong.

He peaked in the 1962-63 Championship side, when his striking partnership with Roy Vernon was the bane of First Division defences.

Young scored 22 goals, and created countless more for his skipper, as Everton claimed their sixth League title.

He was also an integral member of the 1966 FA Cup-winning side, the team which became the first to pull back a 2-0 deficit to win at Wembley.

And Evertonians who study the video tape of that match today are still puzzled as to why he wasn't awarded a first-half penalty!

Despite suffering painfully from blistered feet throughout his playing career, Young amassed 273 appearances for Everton.

His goals return of 87 in those matches was more than respectable - but it was his almost mythical appeal, rather than mere statistical successes, which endeared him to the Everton supporters.

He left Goodison to become player-manager of Irish side Glentoran in 1968, before briefly returning to English football at Stockport County.

Nearly four decades on his adoration amongst Evertonians is undimmed, and his occasional appearances at sporting functions on Merseyside are always packed to capacity.

More than 35 years after he last gracefully glided a ball across Goodison Park, the memory of The Golden Vision is still crystal clear amongst a legion of Blues.

ALEX YOUNG FACTFILE

Born: Loanhead, 1937
Everton Appearances: 273
Everton Goals: 87
Everton Honours: First Division
Championship winner 1962-63
FA Cup winner 1966
FA Charity Shield winner 1963
Scotland caps: 2

'Time after time Latchford would fling himself at the near post to meet a cross'

BOB Latchford was one of the leading goalscorers of his generation – at a time when the dominant force in English football lay on the opposite side of Stanley Park.

But if trophies were out of reach for Evertonians in the 1970s, the very least the long suffering fans needed was a folk hero in the true Royal Blue tradition to allow them to lift their heads in pride.

Bob Latchford became that hero.

He failed to win a single honour during his seven years on Merseyside, but his impact in earning the undying affection of Evertonians, plus his consistently reliable goalscoring record, earned him the 1970s selection ahead of men like Andy King, Mick Lyons and, ironically, Howard Kendall, who moved in the opposite direction to Birmingham City as part of the deal which lured Latchford to Goodison Park.

That package was priced at £350,000 – a British transfer record – placing instant pressure on the broad shoulders of a man recognised as a prolific marksman.

He failed to score on his debut, or even in his next appearance at home to Coventry City. But when he struck with his left-foot at Leicester City, past England goalkeeper Peter Shilton, it sparked a torrent of goals which marked Latchford down as a centre-forward in the Dean, Lawton, Young, Hickson and Royle mould, capable of carrying on the great Everton tradition.

In six successive seasons Latchford topped Everton's club goalscoring charts, but it was the 1977-78 season, when he topped the nation's scoring charts, that Latchford really fired the public imagination.

Concerned by the apparent demise of out-and-out goalscorers, a national newspaper offered a £10,000 prize to the first man to score 30 League goals in a single season.

The previous man to reach such a daunting total had been Manchester City's Francis Lee – seven years previously – who included a record 13 penalty-kicks in his haul.

Aided by the precise crossing skills of Dave Thomas, Latchford reached that total on April 29, 1978.

A last day of the season double against Chelsea secured the prize – with almost perfect timing – just seven days short of the 50th anniversary of Dixie Dean's 60-goal milestone.

His goals that afternoon came from a sharp header and a penalty-kick he had recently been given the responsibility for, in a bid to reach the 30-goal target.

A goal-poacher supreme, many of Latchford's 138 goals for Everton came from close range.

A deceptively quick sprinter over short distances, the burly six-footer possessed the uncanny ability to hang in the air to meet a cross – never better exemplified than in scoring the winning goal in the 1977 League Cup semi-final at Bolton Wanderers.

But diving headers were his speciality.

Time after time Latchford would fling himself at the near post to meet a driven cross – and with one flick of his forehead send the ball arrowing into the opposite corner of the net, the goalkeeper completely foxed.

The dramatic extra-time equaliser at Elland Road in an FA Cup semi-final against West Ham was typical.

Billy Wright's driven cross carried sufficient power to have flashed across the penalty area before most strikers could have blinked.

Latchford, however, plunged to meet the ball with his head and arrowed a perfectly-placed header into the Hammers' net.

Typical of Everton and Latchford's fortunes in that era, West Ham swept straight back down to the opposite end of the pitch to snatch a scrappy winner.

It was a similar story in the 1977 League Cup final trilogy.

In the only domestic final to go to two replays, Latchford scored a dramatic last-minute equaliser in the first replay at Hillsborough, then opened the scoring against Aston Villa in a second replay at Old Trafford.

Villa came back to end normal time at 2-2, then scored a late extra-time winner.

Until the emergence of Graeme Sharp at Goodison, Latchford lay second only to Dixie Dean in the club's all-time goalscoring charts.

It was his successful fulfillment of that goalscoring legacy which gave him such a notable place in the affections of all Evertonians.

BOB LATCHFORD FACTFILE

Born: Birmingham, 1951
Everton Appearances: 289
Everton Goals: 138
Everton Honour: League Cup runner-up 1976-77
England caps: 12

'Some of the saves he made during the 1980s have passed into Everton folklore'

TO be the best player in your position is the target most professional footballers aim towards. At his best, which was most of the time throughout the 1980s, Neville Southall was the best goalkeeper in the world.

The Millennium Giants panel was swamped with candidates for the 1980s Player of the Decade.

Kevin Ratcliffe is still the most successful captain in the club's history; Graeme Sharp is the club's top post-War marksman.

Peter Reid, Andy Gray and Gary Lineker all had their advocates, but the panel was never seriously swayed away from the claims of the single-minded goalkeeper.

Southall's longevity alone between the Goodison goalposts would have earmarked him as an outstanding candidate. He has played more matches for the club than any other player in Everton history.

But it is his enduring excellence in those matches which have established him as an Everton legend.

"I am a firm believer that you never win trophies without an outstanding goalkeeper," said Howard Kendall.

Southall was between the posts for the most successful spell of silverware collection in the club's history. Some of the saves he made during the trophy-laden days of the 1980s have passed into Everton folklore.

The stunning tip-over from Mark Falco in the final minute of the 1985 match at Tottenham is deservedly famous; so, too, was the scrambling tip around a goalpost of Imre Varadi's effort at Sheffield Wednesday the same season - a save shown over and over again by the BBC in their opening credits to *Match of the Day*.

Graeme Sharp played in both those matches - and had justifiable claims himself to be named as the Millennium Giant for the 1980s. But he was adamant that Southall should be the choice.

Like some other Millennium Giants, Southall actually had claims for inclusion in two decades. He kept goal at Goodison for seven seasons in the 1990s, and was typically defiant in the 1995 FA Cup final victory over Manchester United - his second FA Cup winners' medal collected 11 years after the first.

But it was in the 1980s that Southall was recognised to be at the very peak of his profession.

No.9:   1980-1989

A notorious perfectionist, his natural ability was supplemented by hours and hours spent on the training pitches at Bellefield.

During the famous 1984-85 season he was ever-present and was rewarded with the selection as the Football Writers' Player of the Year.

Many pointed to his ill-timed broken ankle - sustained on international duty for Wales against the Republic of Ireland - as the reason the Toffees just failed in a bid to achieve an incredible double the following season.

It wasn't that understudy Bobby Mimms made any mistakes - he kept six successive clean sheets after stepping in - it was just that Southall was capable of making absolutely unbelievable stops that other goalkeepers were incapable of.

He returned after 11 matches of the following season - and Everton stormed to another championship triumph.

Southall remained at his peak throughout the 1980s and into the early 1990s - but even as his powers diminished slightly with age, he still remained one of the most competent goalkeepers around until finally ending his Everton career in November 1997.

NEVILLE SOUTHALL FACTFILE

Born: Llandudno, 1958
Everton Appearances: 750 (a record)
Everton Goals: 1 (in a penalty shoot-out to settle a Full Members Cup tie against Charlton Athletic)
Everton Honours: First Division Championship winner 1984-85, 1986-87, runner-up 1985-86
FA Cup winner 1984, 1995, runner-up 1985, 1989
European Cup Winners' Cup winner 1984-85
League Cup runner-up 1983-84
FA Charity Shield winner 1984, 1985, 1995
Simod Cup runner-up 1988-89
Zenith Data Systems Cup runner-up 1990-91
Football Writers' Player of the Year 1984-85
Wales caps: 92 (a record)

'He was a player whose defensive excellence earned him respect from everybody'

MOST Everton legends can point to the number of great matches they have produced in Royal Blue, as a testament to their status. It is no exaggeration to suggest that Dave Watson can point to the number of great seasons he has enjoyed at Goodison Park.

After signing from Norwich City in 1986, Watson was a rugged and reliable figure at the heart of Everton's defence, he was an inspirational and exemplary captain, he was both caretaker-boss and coach - but most of all, he was always consistently outstanding.

His performance levels rarely dropped anything below excellent, and he was a unanimous choice as Everton's Millennium Giant of the 1990s.

When Howard Kendall agreed to pay Norwich City £1m for his services in August 1986 - a club record at the time for the Blues - the Canaries' boss Ken Brown wailed: "Losing Dave Watson is like having my right-arm cut off."

Perceived at the time as managerial hyperbole, it soon transpired that the Norwich manager was understating Watson's contribution to a football club.

In his first season at Everton, Watson made 35 League appearances as Everton regained the League Championship they had loaned to Liverpool the previous season.

Strangely, it took the player a little time to win his way into the affections of the discerning Everton supporters. But central defensive partner Kevin Ratcliffe had no doubts.

When Watson took over as captain from the most successful player ever to wear the skipper's armband at Goodison, Ratcliffe described his successor as: "The best centre-half I've ever played with."

More than 20 other central defenders, who have come and gone during Watson's 13 years of service at Everton, would agree.

He won the first of his 12 England caps in the Maracana Stadium against Brazil in 1984 - when England celebrated a rare triumph in South America. The last of his international call-ups came in 1988, but there are plenty of reasons to believe that a succession of England managers dismissed his talents too swiftly.

In the build-up to Euro '96, Watson led a Hong Kong Select XI against Terry Venables' European Championship-bound side.

The Select XI was comprised of a hotch-potch of Hong Kong club players and veteran Premiership stars - and were supposed to give England a morale-boosting send-off by conceding a glut of goals.

Watson, however, has never accepted defeat easily in his life and the Select XI severely embarrassed England's best, only losing 1-0.

That was the summer after Watson proudly ascended the Wembley steps to raise aloft the last major trophy collected by an Everton captain - the FA Cup.

Led in typically inspirational fashion by Watson, the Blues ensured Manchester United ended the 1994-95 campaign empty-handed with an against-the-odds victory at Wembley.

Watson displayed his knack of scoring significant goals along that Wembley trail - with a quarter-final winner against Newcastle United.

He also hammered the winning Goodison goal against Liverpool in 1991, in the fifth round (second replay) of the same competition, and few who witnessed it will forget a 25-yard exocet past the England goalkeeper David Seaman at Highbury in 1995 - with his left foot!

Goals, however, were a bonus from a player whose defensive excellence earned him respect from everybody who played with and against him.

DAVE WATSON FACTFILE

Born: Liverpool, 1961
Everton Appearances: 528
Everton Goals: 38
Everton Honours: First Division
Championship winner 1986-87
FA Cup winner 1995, runner-up 1989
FA Charity Shield winner 1987, 1995
Simod Cup runner-up 1988-89
Zenith Data Systems Cup runner-up
1990-91
England caps: 12 (6 with Everton)

Saluting a hero: Howard Kendall walks out for his testimonial against Athletic Bilbao in 2006

A TOTAL of 13 men have held the honour of managing Everton Football Club.

But when it came to selecting the Manager of the Millennium, the choice was immediately whittled down to two. Harry Catterick and Howard Kendall brought more trophies to Goodison than any of the other post-War managers put together.

Catterick collected two League Championship trophies, an FA Cup, two FA Charity Shields - and during the decade of the 1960s presided over a period of unparalleled

consistency which saw the Blues finish outside the top six in the First Division just once.

Only a very special manager could emulate, let alone surpass, those achievements - but Howard Kendall was such a man. During the 1980s the former club captain helped reshape a team which became the most successful in the club's history.

The Millennium Giants panel was absolutely unanimous that Howard Kendall should be selected as the Manager of the Millennium.

Manager of the Millennium

18 78

NIL SATIS NISI OPTIMUM

Everton

HOWARD KENDALL FACTFILE

Born: Ryton-on-Tyne, 1946
Everton Appearances: 276
Everton Goals: 30
Everton Honours (player): First Division
Championship winner 1969-70
FA Cup runner-up 1968
FA Charity Shield winner 1970
Everton Manager: 1981-1987, 1990-1993,
1997-1998
Everton Honours (manager): First Division
Championship winner 1984-85, 1986-87,
runner-up 1985-86
FA Cup winner 1984,
runner-up 1985, 1986
European Cup Winners Cup winners 1984-85
League Cup runners-up 1983-84
FA Charity Shield winners 1984, 1985
FA Charity Shield shared 1986
Zenith Data Systems Cup runners-up
1990-91
Manager of the Year 1984-85, 1986-87

'Those subsequent spells
could barely hope to come
close to his first glorious
period in charge, but the
fact that he was prepared to
even try showed the depths
of feeling Howard Kendall
had - and still has - for
Everton Football Club'

IN simple, statistical terms, his collection of silverware at Everton is unparalleled.

Two League Championship trophies - one won by the incredible total of 13 points - one FA Cup, two FA Charity Shields (and one shared) - and the first European trophy in Everton's history, the 1985 European Cup Winners' Cup.

In order to create those trophy-winning sides, Kendall proved himself a master wheeler-dealer in the transfer market. He brought Millennium Giants Neville Southall and Dave Watson to Goodison, and pulled off a succession of bargain buys which left other managers scratching their heads in bewilderment.

Andy Gray and Peter Reid were written off as injury prone veterans who had both seen better days. Kendall gave them new leases of life and they helped breathe fire into the belly of his sleeping giant.

Kevin Sheedy was a little-used reserve at Liverpool, until Kendall pulled off an audacious £100,000 swoop and transformed him into one of the most sought-after left-sided midfielders in Europe.

Paul Bracewell and Pat Van den Hauwe were modest acquisitions in the summer and autumn of 1984 - but they helped turn an FA Cup-winning side into an all-conquering unit.

Serving with distinction: The relief of avoiding the dreaded drop in 1998 and (opposite) celebrating a derby goal in 1968

The Everton squad of 1984-85 was easily the most successful in Everton's history. It was arguably one of the strongest in League football. From December 22, 1984, Kendall's men remained unbeaten in three competitions for nearly five months.

They only slipped up in May at Nottingham Forest – after the League Championship had already been captured.

Runners-up in League and Cup the following season, Kendall took the controversial decision to sell Gary Lineker to Barcelona. Scorer of 40 goals in his only season after Kendall had brought him to Goodison, he was transferred for a vast profit to the club.

The benefit wasn't just financial. Kendall's judgement, as well as his business acumen, was backed up utterly.

With Adrian Heath and Graeme Sharp restored to the forward line Everton stormed to another League Championship triumph.

Kendall's motivational skills were often unorthodox, but always inspiring. Before a make-or-break FA Cup tie at Stoke City in 1984 he dispensed with the traditional pre-match pep-talk.

A huge following of more than 5,000 Evertonians had made the trip to the Potteries and Kendall simply opened the dressing room windows to allow his players to hear those supporters singing.

"That's your team-talk," he told his players. "Don't let those fans down."

Everton's 2-0 victory that afternoon was the first on the road to winning the FA Cup and ending a 14-year barren spell of silverware at Goodison.

Kendall's team was only prevented from adding to his European success by the ban on English clubs - a frustration which manifested itself in Kendall accepting an invitation to manage Spanish club Athletic Bilbao in 1987.

Twice, however, he answered the call of Goodison when the club needed him most.

He returned as manager in 1990 before resigning a second time in December 1993 - and in 1997 came back for an unprecedented third period in charge.

Those subsequent spells could barely hope to come close to his first glorious period in charge, but the fact that he was prepared to even try showed the depths of feeling Howard Kendall had - and still has - for Everton Football Club.

As the man himself said in one of his more famous quotations: "You can have love affairs with other football clubs.

"With Everton it's a marriage."

People's Club ideologies

'Everton fans will reward a touch of deftness – from either team'

POLAR opposites. But there's no disguising that the "Dogs of War" and the "School of Science" have both been hugely influential – and successful – ideologies at Goodison Park.

It was in 1928, so legend has it, that Steve Bloomer of Derby County and England said:

"Everton always manage to serve up football of the highest scientific order. They worship at the shrine of craft and science."

His words stuck, and Goodison Park duly became the School of Science.

In real terms, this meant that skill and ability were always prized, so much so that Everton fans will to this day break into spontaneous and prolonged applause to acknowledge and reward a touch of individual or collective deftness – from either team.

It was the Dixie Dean-spearheaded team of 1928 that Bloomer initially christened "scientific." And there was little doubt that that side was a swashbuckling, attack-minded force which worked on the 'we'll score one more goal than you' philosophy.

After scoring more than a century of league goals in 1927-28 – 60 of them from Dixie – they were crowned champions.

Two years later they were relegated. With Dean injured for large chunks of the season, Everton still scored 80 goals, but sadly conceded 92.

CHAPTER 2

The origins of two of the club's infamous monikers

'Alec Troup and Ted Critchley were dazzlingly gifted wingers, Warney Cresswell was a cultured full-back and Dixie Dean, quite simply, was the greatest goalscorer of certainly his generation, perhaps of all-time'

Harry Catterick's 60s sides played with style and panache, with Golden Vision Alex Young a striker of 'matchless grace'

They then embarked on the greatest goal spree the club had ever seen.

Second Division defences were no match for a fit again Dean and company and Everton scored 121 league goals – still a club record – on their way to the Second Division title.

The following season they won the First Division crown with another astonishing haul of 116 strikes and in 1932-33 completed a unique hat-trick by winning the FA Cup, scoring 19 goals in their six ties, including three in the Wembley final.

Alec Troup and Ted Critchley were dazzlingly gifted wingers, Warney Cresswell was a cultured full-back and Dixie Dean, quite simply, was the greatest goalscorer of certainly his generation, perhaps of all-time.

Everton played sublime football, and it was largely successful.

By the time the FA Cup was added to the Goodison trophy cabinet in 1933, another supremely-talented artist had been added to the Blues engine room, the great Joe Mercer.

Possessed of a superb tactical brain and outstanding ability, he was nearing the peak of his powers when a young centre-forward called Tommy Lawton arrived from Burnley. Together they became star pupils in a new School of Science.

But if Lawton and Mercer were A-star students, the most inspiring individuals ever to graduate from the School of Science were still to come.

Bobby Collins burned briefly, but brightly in the Goodison firmament...before a Golden Vision sparkled across the Merseyside skyline.

Few footballers of any era have been idolised to the extent that Alex Young was hero-worshipped by Evertonians. A striker of matchless grace and subtlety, he embodied the School of Science with every elegant pass and every mesmerising dribble.

He peaked during the 1962-63 Championship season, but he was still an Everton striker in 1967, when the final piece of Harry Catterick's jigsaw was put into place. With the signing of Howard Kendall from Preston, the Ball-Harvey-Kendall midfield trio which is still revered 40 years later was in place.

Shuttling the ball about in speedy, intricate patterns – they not only formed the heartbeat of a football team no other English club could live with, they did so with a style and a panache totally in keeping with the club's motto, *Nil Satis Nisi Optimum*. It was a style of football which entranced all who watched it.

The Guardian newspaper's Eric Todd wrote prophetic words in his encapsulation of Everton's 3-1 defeat of Manchester United at Goodison Park early in the 1967-68 season.

'I have no hesitation in suggesting that Everton are on the freehold of real greatness,' he declared.

'They may not cross it this season or even next. But cross it they will. Against United, Everton revealed speed and precision, instinct and purpose. On an occasion as this when teamwork transcends everything, individual appraisal is unfair. Who, however, dare minimise the immaculate display of Wilson, the sheer brilliance of Kendall and Harvey, the artistry of Young, the industry of Ball and the precocity of Royle.'

And this, remember, was the Manchester United of George Best, Bobby Charlton and Denis Law!

Twelve months later, when poor Leicester City were put to the sword at Goodison Park and demolished 7-1, *The Daily Telegraph* was even more fulsome in its praise.

'Everton produced what in any other medium would have ranked as a lasting work of art,' opined R. H.

Golden era: 1984-1987

Williams. 'Poor Leicester had no idea how to cope with Ball, who gets better and better but is merely the fulcrum of the team that seems certain to win the championship in a year or two, if not sooner.'

Everton did win the title, around 18 months after Williams' prediction, and they did so in the same style that had fans purring about the School of Science once again. It was a team unmatched at Goodison for 14 years, until two of those midfield maestros took the reins of the club and formed a football team in their own image.

Howard Kendall was the manager and Colin Harvey his assistant during the most successful era in the club's history.

Two league titles, an FA Cup and the club's first-ever European trophy were landed between 1984 and 1987 – with Evertonians showing they hadn't forgotten how to celebrate after 14 barren years. Those same fans also showed they are nothing, if not versatile.

When another favourite son from the 60s School of Science took over at Goodison, Joe Royle, he was forced to employ a different stategy at a time of trial. And Evertonians embraced the idea enthusiastically.

Under Mike Walker Everton had made the worst start to a season in the club's history. After they had parted company, Joe Royle arrived with a reputation as a football firefighter and a very simple mandate – keep Everton in the Premiership.

So was born, the Dogs of War.

"We had to change and quickly," explained Royle. "I'd looked at tapes of Everton, and I felt that they'd been playing 'pretty' football at times, but not being strong enough to withstand the more physical side of the game in a very physical division.

"So I was determined to get people in, people like Barry Horne, John Ebbrell and Joe Parkinson. Andy Hinchcliffe had been out in the cold, so I was determined to get people like that into the side.

"But equally, Anders Limpar was on his way out, and I'd always been a fan of Anders' talent and I had to find a place for him in the team.

"We wanted to be hard to beat, but we also had to have the cutting edge at the other end.

"They were all fantastic, and added to the experienced players we already had, the likes of Dave Watson, Neville Southall, Paul Rideout, they were all fantastic, and they never let Everton or me down.

"I mentioned the Dogs of War one day in an interview. I was asked about our attitude, and I said it's all very well playing School of Science soccer, and nobody wants that more than me, but we have to be aware of our position in the league – we were rooted to the foot of the Premiership at the time – and I said that at times we might have to have a Dogs of War mentality.

"People kept asking me why Vinny Samways wasn't in the team, and the answer was that the other three were doing so well.

"Quite simply, a lot of them just needed loving. I remember saying to Andy Hinchcliffe in the reserve derby, which was the first game I saw as manager of Everton, why he wasn't playing for England.

"He said: 'Well I'm not even in the Everton team!' So I told him that I'd take care of that aspect, so why isn't he playing for England?

"He was that talented, and Andy, if you look back at tapes of that season, the contribution from him was immense.

"The deliveries into the box, he was quick, he was powerful, and with as good a left foot as you'll see, and Andy deserves an awful lot of praise for his input that season – as indeed they all do."

The Dogs of War revived Everton's faltering fortunes – and also embarked upon a stirring FA Cup run which took the club all the way to Wembley.

Manchester United stood between the Blues and silverware – and ahead of the Cup final one-time United fan Joe Parkinson issued a stirring battle cry.

"We have got to get stuck into them because they don't like that," he declared. "They are a team that can dish it out, but they don't like it when they are on the receiving end."

The Red Devils' reply, articulated (if that is right word) by Roy Keane, was: "If it does get physical, we will be ready for it."

There was only one team ready for the fight, however, and Everton triumphed thanks to Paul Rideout's precisely-dispatched header.

It was a triumph for the Dogs of War against Cruft's Best of Breed…

On the way to Wembley: A fan can't contain his excitement in 1995

People's Club Reporting

CHAPTER 3

Original newspaper
writing from some
unforgettable games

Everton

'Scenes? My bonny boy, scenes isn't the word for what will happen ...'

FOOTBALL'S ability to divert and distract the population was never in greater need than throughout the winter of 1914 and the spring of 1915.

With millions of men making the ultimate sacrifice on foreign soil, football fields became key platforms for extolling patriotism and recruiting soldiers.

The FA Cup final of 1915 became known as the 'Khaki Cup Final', such were the numbers of eager young conscripts in the crowd – and Lord Derby did not miss a cue when he presented the Cup to Sheffield United and declared: "You have played with one another and against one another for the Cup. It is now the duty of everyone to join with each other and play a sterner game for England."

The message of unity was never more evident than on Merseyside, where Everton claimed their second League Championship – and their first for 24 years – with a little help from their Stanley Park neighbours.

After making the title running for much of the season, back-to-back home defeats by Burnley and Sheffield Wednesday over Easter had seen Everton hand the initiative to Oldham Athletic.

But when the pressure began to tell, the Latics cracked. Their campaign concluded with home games against Burnley and Liverpool, and the *Liverpool Echo* reported Oldham's results with relish.

'Everton's players were all agog with excitement on Tuesday night upon learning that Burnley were leading 1-0 at Boundary Park,' it reported.

'One famous player indeed rose at 6am on Wednesday to hear the result.

'A draw by Liverpool today at Oldham would suffice locals to the full.'

Everton were not in action on the final Saturday of the season, opponents Chelsea being otherwise engaged in that Khaki Cup Final.

The Toffees went into the weekend level on points with Oldham, but with a far superior goal average (as was used prior to 1976). An Oldham victory over the Reds would have left Everton needing to beat Chelsea at Goodison Park on the following Monday evening – and the *Echo* was already previewing a potential title decider with some excitement.

'It will be a game worth seeing and I'll wager that one of the biggest crowds of the season will see it,' wrote Burns Campbell.

'There will be some scenes if Everton win. Scenes? My bonny boy, scenes isn't the word for what will happen! There will be Tom Watson and Will Cuff shedding tears down each other's back; Lowe and Fleetwood cuddling each other in the middle of the pitch; Parker and Cooper of Barnsley will chance a two-step; and Jack Taylor and Bert Freeman will be there to place crowns of laurels on blushing brows. It will be some night!'

In the event, it was a total anti-climax! Liverpool won 2-0 against a deflated Oldham in front of a meagre gate of 5,080.

'The Anfielders did a kind and neighbourly act at Boundary Park on Saturday, when they defeated Oldham Athletic and incidentally assisted Everton to secure the League Championship,' reported Monday's *Echo*, before adding a hastily compiled ditty:

Tune up the harp; bring forth the bays;
The victors see advancing!
Whose fame the loudest tongue of praise
Must sing in strains entrancing.

To those keen Blades who took the Bun
And changed its current sadly
Let Final honour, finely won
To-day be rendered gladly

To Everton who snatched from fate
(With Liverpool abetting)
The laurels when it looked too late –
When hopes bright sun seemed setting

To Blues, who're League-ally elate
We'll offer as we oughter
Congrats, for which they've had to wait
A century's full quarter!

But the Monday night visit of Chelsea wasn't completely pointless; the visitors were still desperate for

TITLE CLIMAX

EVERTON 2, CHELSEA 2
First Division, April 26, 1915

The Liverpool Echo

Left to right: Tom Fleetwood and Sam Chedgzoy, members of the 1914-15 title-winning side

points to avoid relegation. Tuesday's *Echo* reported: 'The two teams received a hearty reception from the crowd of 10,000 spectators. Chelsea played in a manner directly opposite to Saturday's exhibition and their shooting was sharp and true.

'In nine minutes Brittain scored. Croal and Brittain dovetailed finely and the latter's first-time shot had so sound a goalkeeper as Fern well beaten.

'Everton were greatly surprised and set about their rivals. Kirsopp drove at the goalkeeper and much more troublesome was a solo by Parker, whose effort was clipped by a trip. However, at half-time, Chelsea were value for their lead.

'Everton set a fast pace on the resumption and matters were put on a level peg when Fleetwood scored a fine goal 20 minutes from the finish.

'Fleetwood, tired of waiting for his forwards to test Molyneux, and threading his way through, beat the Chelsea goalkeeper with a fast cross-shot – a popular goal and one hailed with rare enthusiasm.

'Twelve minutes from the finish Ford gave Galt some yards in a spring and when the winger turned inward he was brought down by Galt, Logan netting the penalty-kick. Only a minute passed and then Everton equalised from a corner, Parker hooking the ball into the net in an amazing manner.

'The pace imparted on the ball was simply astounding because the ball was high up when Parker got his boot to it. One of the best goals of the season, it deserved to be put on the same level as Parker's goal against Oldham.

'Everton went tenaciously for the lead and Clennell was a trifle wide with a swift shot. It was a capital wind up to the season and at the last gasp might have ended with a goal, a McNeil drive being perilously near. Everton's best were Fleetwood, Thompson, Clennell and Harrison.'

Chelsea couldn't repeat their performance in Nottingham a couple of days later and were relegated. But for Everton, the title win was placed in context by the local press.

'The Championship means for you, a Cup', explained the *Echo* '13 gold medals – 11 for the players and one each for Mr Will Cuff and Jack Elliott, and £275 to be divided at the rate of 13s 1 and a half d (pence) per match among all the players who have assisted Everton in their League games. The long competition is, of course, more meritorious than the short FA Cup one.'

MATCH STATS

EVERTON: Fern, Thompson, Weller, Fleetwood, Galt, Grenyer, Chedgzoy, Jefferis, Parker, Clennell, Harrison.

CHELSEA: Molyneux, Betteridge, Harrow, Taylor, Logan, Abrams, Ford, Halse, Brittain, Croal, McNeil.

**GOALS: EVERTON Fleetwood (70), Parker (79)
CHELSEA Brittain (9), Logan (78 pen)
ATTENDANCE 30,000 (10,000 according to report)**

'There's never been such a joyful shout at Everton ... it went on for minutes'

IT is perhaps the single most celebrated football match in Everton's long and colourful history. It is certainly the most famous, even if there are only a handful of supporters still around who were there.

It was May 5, 1928 – the day Dixie Dean passed from folk hero into folklore.

Against Arsenal, at approximately 10 to five (the match kicked off at 3.15pm), Dixie Dean scored his 60th League goal of an incredible campaign.

No other player had even come close to recording such a top-flight tally, certainly no-one has come close since – and Dean even eclipsed the record set the previous season in the Second Division.

No moving pictures exist of the occasion. In fact, only one, grainy shadowy photograph has ever been printed purporting to be the moment Dean headed his 60th.

But the *Football Echo* tried to create a picture in words – more than 2,000 of them – of that historic afternoon.

And for the first time since 1928 we have reproduced a full, unedited report of that afternoon's incredible events.

It makes intriguing reading – and paints a marvellous picture of a memorable afternoon.

HOW THEY LINED UP

EVERTON
Davies
Cresswell   O'Donnell
Kelly   Hart   Virr
Critchley Martin Dean Weldon Troup

Peel   Brain Shaw Buchan Hulme
Blyth   Butler   Baker
John   Parker
Paterson

ARSENAL

'Magnificent weather graced the final act of the 1927-28 season at Goodison Park today, when Arsenal visited Everton in a match that promised to be historic, because it meant Everton stood No. 1 in the League after starting No. 1 in the League on August 26 last year.

'It was Charlie Buchan's final match in football history.

'It was Everton's third league championship, it was Dean's best season ever, and opened the possibility of Dean breaking all English League records by getting three goals today.

'Thus the game had many aspects and much appeal. It was not surprising that 50,000 spectators looked at the handsome league trophy that was in the centre of the

directors' box.

'There was a gentle breeze, much animation and an increase in the police force, the last named being charged to keep the crowd from running across the pitch at the end of the game when the presentation was being made.

'An entrance from Bullens Road had been erected for the first time in the history of the club so that mounted police could be brought into the ground at any given moment they were required.

'A spectator shouted to the Everton officials: "Where are the colours?" Everton acted on the hint. Mr Tom McIntosh, their secretary, tying the club colours on the trophy.

'Mr W C Cuff, the chairman, opened proceedings by asking the crowd, through the microphone, to keep their places after the match.

'There was a stupendous cheer for Cresswell and his men and the warmth of the welcome for Buchan showed the public appreciated a famous player.

'Buchan and Cresswell each left Sunderland's service and each has repaid his purchase with grand football.

'Referee W P Harper of Stourbridge gave Dean a hearty hand-grip, and then all was in readiness for the day's pleasure.

'All eyes were glued on the middle patch. It was as though 60,000 spectators were chanting the chorus: "We want you to get goals today," so that the first time Dean went down he had the crowd at his back.

'But he did not score, and moreover the Arsenal went away to score in a manner that set the spectators ablaze.

'Shaw scored in two minutes after handling the ball and "getting away with it" but, remarkable to relate, the ball went through the goalkeeper's hands into the net.

'There was no real pace on the ball, and naturally a shock such as this rather upset the preconceived notions of the Saturday celebrators. However, it was left to the man of the moment to create another sensational and memorable feat.

'Before three minutes had gone Dean had scored two goals, which brought his total to 59, thus equalling Camsell of Middlesbrough who took 59 in Second Division series.

'The crowd's roar knew no bounds. They were crazy after this inspiring turn round on the score sheet.

'It was all very simple in the making. The first point was from a corner taken by Critchley. Martin turned the ball onto Dean, who headed it to the extreme left-hand corner. This was the second chapter at the second minute.

'The third excelled all others. Dean was running through when Butler crossed him. It was an accidental collision - to the referee it was a trip, and the consequence was that Dean was able to rise from the ground and take the penalty-kick successfully and well.

'Three goals in the first five minutes of this championship act was all to the joy of the crowd. It was a fitting start to a fatal game - fatal in the sense that Dean was now wanting but one goal to put him top of England in the league section in the course of 40-odd years of League football.

'Moreover, these goals to Everton meant that Everton were nearing the magic figure of 104 made by West Bromwich Albion soon after the War, the total now being 101.

'Thus the well primed football fan was having a bean feast of figures, fun, facts and fancies.

'In addition, the early play was thrilling and enthralling. For instance, Paterson the Arsenal goalkeeper, patted down a hot one from Dean, and Dean followed up with a charge that nearly sent the long and ungainly-looking goalkeeper into the net.

'Weldon also was close and although Hulme and Buchan came spasmodically with football dodgery, Everton were the more convincing, and Troup in particular had an enjoyable time against Parker.

'This was the third meeting this season of Arsenal and Everton. The first was on Christmas Eve, when Arsenal won the League match 3-2; the next was a Cup-tie three weeks later, when Everton lost by one goal, scored in the last minute, and were described by the London Press as being most unfortunate losers.

DIXIE'S 60

EVERTON 3, ARSENAL 3
First Division, May 5, 1928

Report by 'Bee'

'These meetings between London and the Lancashire side had thus produced more than the average crop of goals. Just to show that he was human, Dean shot outside when unmarked, when he knew he was offside.

'Arsenal, with the wind behind, then had an incisive way of attacking and Hulme was going strong until the rugged O'Donnell covered his centre and stopped the possibility of another goal.

'In return Virr attempted a swinging shot after Kelly had duffed a free-kick, and next came a wonderful screw centre by Hulme to Shaw, who followed up so well that he made the goalkeeper Davies drop the ball and go to earth.

'Dean was at his best when he chased back towards his own half and headed a ball, in spite of Parker's attention. Troup followed this move with an equally brilliant move and Arsenal, through Buchan and Shaw, also added the pleasantries of the day with football of an artistic character.

'Hulme and Shaw made one of the best duo turns of the match with the result that the flight ball was put towards the dusty road towards goal, and Davies, for the third time, picked up with indecision.

'Hart was doing famous work at centre-half so that Butler, his rival, when forced to kick away, came near putting the ball through his own goal. No half-back played quite so well as John.

'There were a fair number of offside decisions against Dean, through Parker and company racing forward. But another anti-climax in the game came when O'Donnell heeled the ball through his own goal. This was the second defensive blunder on the part of the home man and its cost was big.

'The situation was quite simple and Davies was about to pick up the ball when O'Donnell crossed him and, in the mix-up, O'Donnell turned the ball over his own goal-line.

'Fortunately the result did not matter but, remembering that each blunder meant a goal, led the spectators into a rather sombre state of mind.

'Right on half-time Shaw made a jolly run and crossed the ball over the mouth of the goal without getting reward, and Troup produced some of his fireworks which must have produced a goal for Dean had he sighted the ball.

'The home centre, however, lost the flight of the ball and chance of a lifetime to make his record.

'Half-time: Everton 2, Arsenal 2.

'In the second half the tension was naturally increased, especially as the Arsenal continued to play charming football and Blyth had a fine understanding with Peel.

'The home captain covered up the ex-Yorkshire player in a way that had been foreign to him (Peel) in previous meetings this season.

'Dean strove upward and onward, and although he angled awkwardly he got full power onto the spinning ball so that Paterson's save at the foot of the post was a brilliant one.

'The wind did not prevent the air being sultry and naturally the pace began to slacken a bit.

'However, the home centre-forward was not greedy about goals, and at this point he offered Critchley a pass and the little man knocked a hot shot against the angle of the goalpost. Davies, at the other end, made a good, confident punch-away and Baker lifted the ball into the number board.

'Everton were facing the sun, facing odds, and playing a trifle too hard so that the game travelled anybody's way and the crowd of possibly 60,000 was kept on tenterhooks and for the moment had to be content to watch the excellence of Weldon, Virr and company.

'For long spells Dean was crowded out, or received unwise passes, and at the hour he broke through and seemed an assured scorer when the ball swung a yard outside. Time was flying and the crowd now got really hearty over the main issue of the day – namely Dean's need for one goal!

THE **MATCH REPORTS**

'This was the beginning of Dean's historic record goal in English football. Troup took the corner kick and out of a ruck of probably 14 players, Dean, with unerring accuracy, nodded the ball to the extreme right hand side of the goal'

'A lovely ankle pass from Dean to Troup led to instant response by Troup, whose centre was headed no more than six inches over the crossbar. One had to be present to feel the sighs of the crowd during the tense moments of the Everton attack. The ball was lively and that must have been the cause of Dean now making a left-foot effort that should have been an easy goal instead of travelling far and wide.

'Hulme, England's outside-right, had suffered one of those blank days which come to everyone in turn. Dean had the right idea in a breakaway, but overran the ball and thus another half-chance went away.

'There was an unusual stoppage through the Arsenal goalkeeper having dust in his eye.

'After Arsenal had come near scoring Critchley put the ball out to Troup who fired a diagonal shot that knocked out a child spectator of 10 years. Ambulance men attended to the youngster, who was soon all right.

'Brain missed a useful chance from a corner and the longer time sped on the more certain it appeared that Dean and the others had run themselves dry in an excess of endeavour.

'Still, one had to appreciate the sterling qualities of Butler, who had headed the ball more often than any man on the field.

'Something of the Nerve and Knox comedy element entered into the play when big Parker stood statuesque and headed away from the wee Troup, who stood immediately underneath him.

'Weldon came near taking the lead with a ball that cannoned off a defender. With nine minutes to go the crowd yearned for a goal to Dean or anyone and nearly got their voices working when Martin shot and Paterson punched away over the bar for a corner-kick.

'This was the beginning of Dean's historic record goal in English football. Troup took the corner-kick and out of a ruck of probably 14 players, Dean, with unerring accuracy, nodded the ball to the extreme right-hand side of the goal.

'There has never been such a joyful shout at Everton.

'It was prolonged for minutes and went on to the end of the game. The crowd never stopped cheering for eight solid minutes and Dean was hugged by all his comrades and, indeed, there was a threat of the crowd breaking onto the field of play.

'In fact two men rushed across through the barrier of police, and the referee had to bundle one man off and out of the way of trouble.

'It was a memorable scene, and was followed by another sample of nervous strain, such as one has become accustomed to in Cup finals. A very simple position was created by Peel and Davies, having got his hands and chest to the ball, should have made an easy save. The home goalkeeper was off his game, however, and when the ball struck the near upright and cannoned out to Shaw there was no-one to stop the Arsenal scoring.

'Davies took off his cap and scratched his head in greater wonderment than anyone on the field.

'There were curious interludes before the finish, Paterson, the Arsenal goalkeeper, making a catch at the top of the bar, and when the referee gave a corner-kick he protested loud and long that the referee had erred.

'The goalkeeper went back to his place accepting the referee's decision and giving Dean a shake of the hand, a sporting act fitly recognised by the crowd.

'A moment later, while the corner-kick was being taken, Butler took the opportunity of congratulating Dean. In a minute the whistle had gone for the final, O'Donnell had carried off the ball and the crowd settled themselves down to listen to the speech of Mr John McKenna, English League President, who presented the trophy to Cresswell amid roysterous cheers.

'The amplifiers did their best to make the speech of the presenter heard, but it could not be said that they were very successful.

'And that's how Everton wound up the season and ended their memorable year of office.

'At the end of the match Mr W C Cuff, chairman of the club, whose voice carried well over the microphone, congratulated the side upon its victory, in what he described as the most wonderful season the game of football has ever known.'

MATCH STATS

EVERTON: Davies, Cresswell, O'Donnell, Kelly, Hart, Virr, Critchley, Martin, Dean, Weldon, Troup.

ARSENAL: Paterson, Parker, John, Baker, Butler, Blyth, Hulme, Buchan, Shaw, Brain, Peel.

**GOALS: EVERTON Dean (3, 5 pen, 81)
ARSENAL Shaw (2, 89), O'Donnell (35, o.g.)
ATTENDANCE 48,715**

'It was a happy day for citizens of Liverpool and the followers of Everton FC'

EVERTON'S 1933 FA Cup triumph – the Toffees' first at Wembley – was the first time the most recognisable silverware in English football history had graced the Goodison trophy cabinet.

The original FA Cup was stolen from a Birmingham shop window on September 11, 1895 and an exact replica – won by the Blues in 1906 – was presented to Lord Kinnaird in 1910.

A whole new design, the one still used today, was first presented in 1911 to Bradford City.

It was won for the first time by Everton in 1933, and despite a 27-year wait since their last outing to the capital, Evertonians showed they hadn't forgotten how to celebrate.

The *Liverpool Daily Post* reported the post-match celebrations following Everton's 3-0 defeat of Manchester City.

'The West End of London was thronged at night with a crowd that seemed to have gone completely patriotic, the red, white and blue colours of the fans of Everton and Manchester City blending in a sporting harmony.

'Crowds of happy-go-lucky football fans from every part of the country came by train, bus and tube to the West-end as soon as the Stadium game ended and there they besieged cafes and restaurants to fortify themselves for a nocturnal sight-seeing tour or a theatre.

'But the centre of London's Cup night celebration was the Hotel Victoria, where Everton dined and danced.

'A crowd gave the team a boisterous reception when Dean, clasping the Cup in his arms, led them into the hotel and the staff continued the welcome inside.' As ever, the *Liverpool Echo's* august correspondent "Bee" captured the occasion in painstaking detail and no little colour. His report is faithfully reproduced here:

A RECORD HAT-TRICK BY THE BLUES

How the Great Victory Was Won

Goals By Stein, Dean and Dunn
Manchester City Outclassed

'Everton's victory at Wembley on Saturday was one of the easiest in recent Cup finals. By three goals to nothing Everton beat Manchester City and won the Cup for the second time in the history of the club, and completed a record which may never be equalled, that of winning the Second Division Championship, the First Division Championship and the Cup in successive years, which in these days of keen competition is a remarkable "hat-trick" of honours.

'Everton thoroughly deserved their victory. The goals were scored by Stein, Dean and Dunn and the whole side played cool, calculating football. On the other hand, the City defence was very shaky almost from the beginning. The numbering of the players for the first time in a final tie was greatly appreciated by the spectators.'

By Bee

'EVERTON FC are on their way rejoicing. They bring with them the Football Association Cup that evaded them since 1906, when they beat Newcastle by one goal.

'They went two better at Wembley on Saturday before nearly a hundred thousand people, in perfect weather and a setting that was extremely beautiful, graced as it was by the Duke of York (the King was unable to be present) and nothing more remains but the homecoming per Lime Street Station, just before eight o' clock tonight and the civic reception at the Town Hall, after which the winning team will wend its way – wend is the right term in the circumstances – to Goodison Park, there to meet enthusiastic Everton followers, the ground being thrown open and music being provided.

'My task just now is to review the match and I am doing so without having seen or heard anyone's opinion.

'It is better that way, because one may easily fall by inference or interference through communication with other onlookers.

'My view uninterrupted leads me to say at once that there could be no possible shadow of doubt the better side winning. The margin was not unkind to Manchester City; they deserved their second half endeavour, but Everton by then had made the issue safe, and by what methods? Just the good old fashioned methods of playing altogether, not as units.

'When Manchester City sped off they did so through two main avenues and one back street (McMullan's subtly). They had to depend on the racing raids of Brook and Toseland.

'Everton, on the other hand, played well together; it was everybody's job to help the other comrade: there was not one outstanding individualistic run; not one solo among 11 members, all performing in the same pleasant suit; it was all round ability and blend that won this game, and a steady refusal to be rattled into the nervy state by the wild rushing of the City forwards. Let me state at once that the game took three distinct turns and leanings.

'First it was City's attack that prevailed without a shot of note: then it became all Everton right up to half-time. On the resumption Everton again took command, but finally having obtained a lead that needed three for the other side to overthrow, the leaders Everton merely awaited the final whistle.

'And Manchester City wound up on a note of fiery endeavour that was mere prattle; they were like the child that was "always going to." They never kept their word and did not keep their promise.

'In the second half they must have been on the attack for the best part of 25 minutes and they merely beat themselves against the well-planned defence trinity. This could not be a wildly exciting game to the onlooker who

WEMBLEY FIRST

EVERTON 3, MANCHESTER C. 0
FA Cup final, April 29, 1933

Report by 'Bee'

Cup Final Remembrances—By George Green

FINAL TIT-BITS WE SHALL NEVER FORGET.

SO THIS IS WEMBLEY

DO I LOOK LIKE MAURICE CHEVALIER?

'DIXIE' DEAN'S STRAW HAT.

GEORGE GREEN .33.

BANG!

THE FARE SERVED·UP BY EVERTON'S COOK.

WARNEY CRESSWELL'S SANG FROID.

THE PART PLAYED BY GREAT BRITTON.

HELP!

THOSE CURLY CORNERS BY JIMMY STEIN.

THE HALF A MILLION PEOPLE WHO TURNED OUT TO WELCOME THE CUP! CAN YOU IMAGINE HALF A MILLION PEOPLE? I HOPE YOU CAN BECAUSE I HAVEN'T TIME TO DRAW THEM ALL.

An Echo cartoon by George Green tells the story of the 1933 FA Cup final

had not come from either Manchester or Liverpool; the reason for the lack of special thrill was that the goals were close ups in each case; that Manchester City were made to be disappointing by the all-round excellence of Everton.

'City were as good as Everton allowed them to be; and that goodness was mainly concealed into spasms of attacking raids which bore no finality and never looked like producing tangible result.

'No, Everton were masters of this game as soon as the City goalkeeper had blundered into upper-cutting a ball with his hands when he might have edged it over the bar; later Langford made the same error. He was watching a corner-kick and stretching out his hand he barely brushed the ball, which went to the net aided by the ever-attentive Dean, than whom there is no forward quite so good in timing his heading, charging or gauging an onside position. The game could not be one long thrill with the winners dominating the game to a degree rarely seen in Cup finals.

'Actually, Everton have broken Wembley records by scoring the clearest victory, 3-0, and at this stage it is well we should study the make up of the goals.

'The first came to Stein in 40 minutes. Every Everton follower had a notion that if Everton were to win they must have a leading goal from Stein, who had become the shooter-in-chief, while others had rather gone out of the fashion of making goals.

'Stein had already had one shot at City's goalkeeper, and the latter saved by the device of dropping to his knees and though the ball with its hot pace escaped his vigilant hands, it travelled onto the buffer of Langford's body. Britton swung across a hanging centre and Stein, having closed in, the Manchester defence was near breaking point. For this reason Langford looked for attention from Dean, and the backs bothered the goalkeeper, but left a gap so that Stein could use his right foot and towering over the left hand of the goal space, drive home a fast shot.

'One goal often suffices in Cup finals, but last year Newcastle won after being a goal down. So Everton realised that they must keep up their pressure, which had been sustained upon the uncertain backs and goalkeeper from the 20th minute to the 45th minute, which was the retiring period.

'Now Manchester City had the sun at their backs (Dean had started right by winning the toss and having the sun at his back), and Manchester showed a spurt that looked compelling till it came to the path of Cresswell or Cook or Sagar's safe hands.

'In seven minutes the issue had been settled.

'Britton took a throw-in, feinted to move this way and that way, and finally sent in his second successful lob – bowler's length. Dean seized this as a scoring chance. Again, Langford reached out one hand towards the ball that was beating him and one eye upon Dean. Actually,

Dean charged his foeman fairly and squarely and I verily believe the ball was just over the line when Langford took a seat, lying flat, and Dean brushed the ball into the net.

'This was a decisive factor, with Britton as the workman, and a forward as the man with the finishing touch.

'Dean had missed such a chance in the first half that he would relish this redeeming goal. The goal had been gaping at him; Dean had to whiff the ball to the back of the net with his foot, his knee or his chest. Dean raised his right foot to attain his object and the ball passed under the back of his knee! The crowd was stunned; Manchester was "much obliged" and felt it was some consolation for the absence of their crack centre-forward Tilson, who could not play in this game and was unable to play as a schoolboy international and as an English international through the same cause – injury. However, Everton two-up and 38 minutes to go were content to trust themselves and their defence.

'For a long time the game took a decided Manchester reign; with the same inefficiency near goal, with the same slicing of the ball by wingers, and the ragged half-back play that had obtained where skill was supposed to be at its highest point. I do not remember a team falling away so quickly and so definitely as Manchester City.

'The first came to Stein in 40 minutes. Every Everton follower had a notion that if Everton were to win they must have a leading goal from Stein, who had become the shooter-in-chief, while others had rather gone out of the fashion of making goals'

'McMullan started like an artist and finished a tired man; Busby started brilliant with scientific moods and moves; and Bray was throughout the complete half-back, but he stood alone in this matter and only Brooks and Toseland showed up in the other regions, Marshall being a spent force and Herd, tried at centre-forward, ploughing a lonely field and doing best with his head, but being utterly unable to get through the avenue that was surrounded by White, Cresswell and Cook.

'City piled on pressure and pace without finality; the more they tried the more they broke their own curbed belief; thay ran into the clinches; they were easy prey for two men of direct, opposite tastes in defence; Cook the lover of the lusty kick and Cresswell the fine art dealer who with his head and toe took all raids with special pleasures. He shattered them all.

'City, on the other hand, went in for a lot of nervy play; it was poor football brains because they lost this final tie, in my judgement, through the stress they brought on themselves by giving away corner-kicks.

'In the first half they conceded so many that they came to fear Stein's trusty centre. Stein has a partnership with Johnson in these matters. Johnson lies in front of the goalkeeper and Stein applies a certain amount of hook to his delivery.

'As the corner is taken Johnson either ducks his head or runs slightly forward and thus distracts the goalkeeper's attention. Corner-kicks have had so little value for 40 years that one must applaud any players who make good use of the free-kicks.

'Stein was a model corner-kick taker and he had so many chances to display his accuracy that the City defence started to make and take up positions that were not warranted; Cann began worst and Dale followed him as time went on. So Manchester courted defeat by the over-plus pressure of corner-kicks taken with due regard to sense of direction and strength. The third goal was quite the prettiest of the lot and served to save Geldard, perchance, some of the biting criticism that comes to those who conquer.

'Geldard took a corner-kick with a fine touch, and Dunn, the doubtful starter of Friday, got his head to the ball and swung it to the left-hand side of the goal – a picture effort and the concluding item in the Cup agenda.

'Everton had won 3-0 by convincing methods, by their superior craftsmanship, by all-round merit, with hardly a weakness and with a lot of solid work interspersed with the daintier touches of Johnson and Dunn.

'True, this was not sparkling football from the highest angles of criticism, but those who see finalities know the human factor is the biggest winner at Wembley, and certainly Everton played a game that sent Manchester City into hiding; without Everton's delightsome phases and steadiness, this game would have been a thing to forget; Everton saved it by their own merit and excellence.

'Where every man contributed his portion it is irksome to say anything about each player, but I must pay tribute to Sagar's leaping and catching, a faultless display and ticklish when high and awkward shots came between the goalkeeper and the upright; Cook and Cresswell have already been "decorated"; at half-back Britton was

outstanding because he did everything by way of a morsel of artistry. He toyed with the ball just long enough to turn it in the space of a foot or less, and then made his pass or his swinging centre towards goal.

'Britton had no superior, although Busby started remarkably well and Bray was consistency itself.

'Britton was an artist; White closed the middle piece to inside forwards and gave Herd very little chance; Thomson had a task early on in facing the undoubtedly skilful Toseland, and the longer he played the more certain he became.

'Thomson got his tackling grip on the right-wing pair till he covered Marshall right out of the issue. Forward, as elsewhere, one cannot split the side; Dean never headed with more value; Cowan is a big man to face; he has generally won the duels with Dean, but here Dean glided and glanced the ball with rare distinction, and by his side Johnson and Dunn added their strength.

'On the extreme wings there was a quietude one doesn't expect. Geldard had his inspired moments, but he was generally crowded out through delaying his final move. Stein, always a matchwinner, was kept idle for long stretches but in the first half showed unmistakably how he had rattled the City defence.

'Stein had not one of his spectacular "running" days any more than Geldard had his share; the truth was that the ball did not go that way to any degree.

'This match was won through team spirit and consistent endeavour through the combined measures; Manchester City's method of dash and grab has been insufficient against a defence that was so strong, none being better than Cresswell.

'Nervous strain ran through the losers' defence; confidence reigned supreme in the Everton side.

'They had their shaky moments in earlier rounds at Goodison Park; having got to the final tie they seemed to feel relieved and they never gave a trace of losing their nerve. Worthy winners, therefore, by a margin that was justified by the way the various ranks played.

'After 27 years Everton bring back the Cup. They started at Leicester in the opening round; that day Stein, Dean and Dunn scored.

'So they merely began as they intended to go on. And in the final tie they ended as they had begun with goals to Stein, Dean and Dunn.'

MATCH STATS

EVERTON: Sagar, Cook, Cresswell, Britton, White, Thomson, Geldard, Dunn, Dean, Johnson, Stein.

MANCHESTER CITY: Langford, Cann, Dale, Busby, Cowan, Bray, Toseland, Marshall, Herd, McMullen, Brook.

GOALS: EVERTON Stein (40), Dean (52), Dunn (80)
ATTENDANCE 92,900

'We're extremely proud of our treble honour'

IN an early example of post-match interviews, the *Echo* reported the views of both captains.

City captain Sam Cowan said: "We felt when we were a goal down that we had quite a reasonable chance of drawing level, if not of winning, but that second goal did the trick. It was a crushing blow and all our boys failed to produce their best form. We know that and feel it. We do not want to hide it, but we must say that your players kept a cool head and played very good football indeed in every department. There was not a weakness."

Dean, in thanking Cowan, said: "If the Cup is to go out of our keeping, we hope you will be the winners. There could be no doubt about the issue, I think, because speaking apart from myself, there was not a weakness anywhere. Our fellows were very confident and they kept together well. I think the turf was magnificent and suited our tactics, and while we sympathise with you, of course, you will understand we are extremely proud of the treble honour of the First Division, Second Division and the Cup in successive years.

"I don't think that record will ever be equalled, chiefly because the winning of the Second Division Championship and the next year the First Division is so uncommon. It has only been done by Liverpool and Everton. When you take in the Cup as the third and final effort, well, really it is a miracle, isn't it?"

'Thrill packed upon thrill; incident upon incident ... it was a match of a lifetime'

TEN goals, a manager 'escorted off the pitch' by the referee, chaotic scenes in and around Goodison Park – and 'a blind man, a boy and a man minus a leg making their exit into the players' tunnel!' – no wonder Everton's 1935 FA Cup classic against Sunderland was described as 'one of the most thrilling in the history of the Cup.'

The two sides had drawn 1-1 at Roker Park the previous Saturday, after sharing 15 goals in 24 hours at Christmas a month earlier.

Sunderland came to Goodison on Christmas Day and were pummelled 6-2, then exacted complete revenge 24 hours later when they triumphed 7-0 at Roker Park – and the buzz around Goodison prior to the Cup replay on January 30 suggested the fans anticipated more fireworks.

The *Daily Post* headline 'Rush to Goodison – Spectators Travel In Hearses' underlined the efforts fans were making to get to the game, played on a Wednesday afternoon.

'The rush to the halfday holiday match at Goodison Park began long before the start, and when the shops closed so great was the demand for transport that every conceivable type of vehicle was brought into service,' reported the *Post*.

EVERTON'S CUP
TRIUMPH

Ten Goals In Two
Hours' Struggle

SUNDERLAND'S
GREAT RALLY

OVER 59,000 THRILLED
BY EPIC GAME

'Taxicabs in a constant stream went backwards and forwards between the ground and the city, the drivers attempting to avoid the traffic jams that occurred by utilising side streets and little known routes. It appeared as though every taxi in the city was being used to take the many thousands to the match.

'The tramcars had long since taken their loads of passengers to the ground and still the crush of vehicles continued. The hansom cab was passed by the latest streamlined limousine, while wagons, carts and even hearses carried their quota of enthusiasts. Added to these were hundreds of motorcyclists and bicycles.

'It must be years since taxicab drivers had such a busy time. Scarcely one of the vehicles could be seen in the city shortly before the game started. Hundreds of them had taken their passengers to the ground, but were requisitioned repeatedly by people on their way to the game, so that it was some time before they were able to return to town.

'Meanwhile, nearly 60,000 people had entered the ground. Several thousands were unable to gain admittance and many remained outside.'

Those that failed to get in missed a match that was talked about for decades.

The redoubtable "Bee" didn't know quite where to start in his summing up of events the next day.

'Everton duly passed to the next round of the Cup by beating Sunderland at home before 59,213 spectators (a gate of £4,382 5s 6d), the score of 6-4 being an uncommon figure and a just one, obtained only after the greatest amount of effort on the part of the Everton team after extra time.

'It was a match of a lifetime; one international player of years gone by told me he had never seen anything to approach this historic struggle. Thrill packed upon thrill; incident upon incident; goal upon goal; a home victory seemingly settled a quarter of an hour from the finish of the 90 minutes only for a rallying force by Sunderland (shocked by two goals margin) fighting back to accomplish the seemingly impossible – two goals in the

10-GOAL THRILLER

EVERTON 6, SUNDERLAND 4
FA Cup fourth-round replay,
January 30, 1935

The Daily Post

Charlie Gee makes his presence felt in the epic tie of 1935

closing stages – the equaliser to bring the score to 3-3 being the most spectacular and strange looking of the ten.

'There were no headed goals; the foot did the trick 10 times and the best goal of all was that which Connor drove home, but picture the Gurney goal which kept the game alive for another half-hour. Time was passing; the tender lead of the home side seemed sufficient; one is enough, if it is one more than the opposing side has scored. Gurney was 10 yards away from goal, his back to the goal; a rather high ball is near him. He can only hook it over his head, but it is beyond Sagar's power to stop it and Gurney hears the roars of a goal he has made and has not seen. It is all so romantic and astonishing that the crowd of city supporters is stunned, while the large party of Sunderland excursionists is renewing its throwing of streamers to make the grand stand look like the festive board of a Christmas party's dining table.

'Half an hour is added to the game; the pace has been killing; one wonders how these players can raise another gallop of checkmate the indisputably able Sunderland forward line.

'The pace does not slacken; though the mud sticks to the leadened ball and the light begins to fail.

'The turning point of this fluctuating game had arrived two minutes after the start of extra time.

'Coulter scored. In those two words one saw the turning of the tide and torrent. This goal, one of the Irishman's three successful efforts at goaltaking served to stun Sunderland and, although Connor, the outstanding forward on the field, equalised the scores at 4-4 a few minutes later with the best shot of the match, Sunderland hardly recovered from the sudden lead two minutes after extra time's big toll had started.

'Finally Geldard took the score to 6-4 and once more a goal had been scored with practically the last kick of time.

'One felt sorry for the losers because they had played beautiful football in attack; their movement was consecutive and convincing; the ball was kept on the ground and was used in draughtsman's manner; there was art and craft in all they did till they reached the vital part of their task; the goal area was reached by such divering ways and in such charming, combined fashion that Sunderland forgot how to polish their medals; their shooting from easy range was, at times, atrocious. They scattered their great gifts before the final act. And they must bear the punishment of their own faults. Still, they

THE **PEOPLE'S** CLUB

CASUALTIES AT GOODISON PARK

AMBULANCE MEN BUSY with minor casualties in the crush at yesterday's Cup-tie between Everton and Sunderland, while the police are endeavouring to prevent spectators from invading the field. — DAILY POST

had, as on Christmas Day, given the spectators a great cup-tie treat, an epic display and a gallant game.

'Everton won through because of their effectiveness near goal. There was an early muddling sort of goal and another not exactly pretty in its frame up, yet all goals count whatever their initial "arrangement" of forces and Everton deserved their victory.

'It was not a hammer and tongs cup tie; it was genuinely good football from start to its rousing finish and at the end of the game the Everton team had difficulty in retracing their steps to the dressing room because the crowd surged onto the playing field and mobbed the players, who had hardly sufficient strength to make their way through any more "opposition."

'In a game of this character the referee is all-important and vital. Saturday's game between the two teams had been spoiled by the tactics adopted by Sunderland. Here, then, came the mighty Football Association making its wise decision to bring in Mr Pinckston of Birmingham, a striking figure of a man cradled in the game at Aston Villa's ground. Mr Pinckston tolerated no fouls, no petty displays of temper, no suggestion of ulterior motives and no tripping. He spoke to a number of players very earnestly and firmly, and one who had kicked the ball away from the spot marked for a free-kick suffered the indignity of being ordered to walk some distance to the referee to receive his admonishment.

'The Sunderland manager Mr Cochrane, a physical mite, entered the field of play when the cessation of 90 minutes had been signalled and was duly escorted from the field by order of the referee.

'Any thought of wasting time – a natural inclination by a tired out team – was brought to book by the referee who earns as much praise as the 22 players who served up the best display of football seen in this city in League or Cup tie match.

'The strain of the game was so intense, so much so

that Cunliffe, it was learned after the game, had played through the last half-hour in a state of semi-consciousness. He had headed a ball and had played by instinct just as Nichol had played when Liverpool were beating Portsmouth a fortnight ago.

'There can be no further individual comment; praise is handed out to every player for a grand exhibition of real football, but one has to pay further tribute to Sagar (early and late in the game), to Connor and to the boy of the game, Stevenson, for general brightness and endeavour and Jones, of Ellesmere Port, who was being tested to the greatest degree and did not fail his side, especially when at one point Gurney was right through the defensive ranks and was prevented taking a goal by the strong and clever and safe young defender.

Now the chart of the goal register:

'Coulter for Everton, 14 minutes;
Coulter for Everton 31 minutes;
Davies for Sunderland 41 minutes;
Stevenson for Everton 75 minutes;
Connor for Sunderland 80 minutes;
Gurney for Sunderland 89 minutes;
Coulter for Everton 2 minutes;
Connor for Sunderland 9 minutes;
Geldard for Everton 21 minutes;
Geldard for Everton 29 minutes.

'The crowd was not nearly a record, but there were attempts to rush the gates, and outside the ground tens of thousands congregated for some time to try to enter into the joy of this joyful game.

'Early on, one of the corners of the ground broke through, and a blind man, a boy and a man minus a leg were seen to make their exit into the players' subway, but by degrees the crowd was replaced in its proper position and the game, thanks to wise control by the police, was never in danger of being interrupted.

'Result: Everton 6, Sunderland 4.'

Yes, that's right. A match which finished 6-4, almost a couple of thousand words of analysis – and the only reference to Dixie Dean came in the teams at the end! It really was an amazing afternoon.

MATCH STATS

EVERTON: Sagar, Cook, Jones, Britton, Gee, Thomson, Geldard, Cunliffe, Dean, Stevenson, Coulter.

SUNDERLAND: Thorne, Murray, Hall, Thomson, Johnston, Hastings, Davis, Carter, Gurney, Gallacher, Connor.

GOALS: EVERTON Coulter (14, 31, 92), Stevenson (75), Geldard (111, 119) SUNDERLAND Davies (41), Connor (80, 99), Gurney (89) ATTENDANCE 59,213

'The derby attendance was recorded at 78,299 - which will never be topped'

NEVER have more people been crammed inside the People's Club than the afternoon of September 18, 1948.

The nation was emerging from the austerity and bleakness of the War Years and the population was desperate for a diversion from the daily grind of a still heavily-rationed daily life.

Football provided that distraction. Attendance records were being smashed nationwide, and when the first Merseyside derby of the 1948-49 season was staged at Goodison Park, an attendance figure never witnessed before or since on Merseyside gathered.

The previous season's Goodison derby had seen 66,766 supporters crammed into the stadium. An FA Cup tie staged at Goodison between Manchester United and Liverpool (United's Old Trafford ground was still heavily bomb damaged) had attracted even more, 74,721. But when old rivals Everton and Liverpool clashed, even that staggering statistic was put into the shade.

The following day's papers recorded the crowd as 78,599. The figure was later amended to 78,299 - a mark which has never been topped, and in these days of all-seater stadia, never will.

In the immediate post-War years however, huge gates were commonplace and only fleeting reference was made to the enormous attendance in the post-match reports. The *Football Echo* reporter "Stork" at least described the scene:

RECORD (78,599) CROWD SEE "OLD FIRM" HOLD RAMPANT REDS FOR 80 MINUTES ... THEN CAME THE GOALS - FAGAN FIRST AND A DODDS PENALTY

DERBY FULL HOUSE

EVERTON 1, LIVERPOOL 1
First Division, September 18, 1948

Reports by 'Stork' and 'Bee'

By Stork

'Everton confounded the critics. Not only had they played grand football, but the "old guard" lasted it out to the bitter end. Perhaps not as good as some Derby games we have seen, because mainly the defences were in command.

'Record for the ground is 74,721, in last season's FA Cup tie between Manchester United and Liverpool, but it was quite possible that these figures would go by the board today, as each section of the ground looked to be well and truly packed and there were many thousands outside.

'There were many casualties and some swaying in parts of the paddock. As is usual in Derby games, the players came out in pairs and it was seen that Stevenson was the Everton captain.'

A more considered, and marginally more concise report was produced in the *Daily Post* by the ubiquitous "Bee", who in the post-War, less security-conscious atmosphere, was now also revealing himself as Ernest Edwards. He wrote:

By Ernest Edwards "Bee"

'The gossamer skeins woven into the Everton-Liverpool texture had vital results, and the memory of the record crowd of 78,599 will be of many featureful incidents. How much depends upon how little was evidenced by "the goals that matter".

'Goals matter so much no-one can estimate the effect of the slightest rub of the Goodison Park green – and how green it was.

'Let me scan some fundamentals.

'The moment Jones left the field to seek trainer's aid, Everton's defensive area was as bare as a bombed site.

'Jones held up play in a manner not common to an injured player who usually drops to earth and awaits the attention of a trainer bowed with care and worry.

'Jones himself now called a halt, went to the touchline and saw a goal taken during his absence. Some may claim he would have served his side better if he had remained on the field wrapped in his mystery injury. The rules say he must go to the line if there is to be a stay of execution.

'The look on the face of the heroic Saunders and Hedley and Sagar when Fagan scored was one of despair. There was really not sufficient time to remedy the damage – or so it seemed, until a strange intervention of fate brought the second goal.

'Sidlow ought have prevented a corner-kick arising. He was watching the ball pass to nothingness when it barely touched the nap of his jersey.

'A corner! People yell for a corner as players yell for a throw-in. Neither count for much once in a hundred times. Everton, battling against age, a deficit and all

Save of his life: Ted Sagar, in action here at Goodison

> ## 'Payne was perky and inclined to ignore the wise, bald pate of Balmer … who called for a cross at Payne's convenience, whereas Payne travelled in and around, scissoring his legs over the ball like a Tisky'

manner of fortuitous circumstances, clung to this straw.

'Boyes and Powell had worked a trick at the corner flag. Powell ran from right to left to take corners: it became a habit and Boyes, by way of variation, stood quite near, took up a pass instead of a centre by Powell.

'This corner brought Boyes a chance to show his irregular tip-toe steps. He shot, Shepherd unmistakably handled and that was how Everton came to their penalty award.

'Everton, having missed penalties, had ordained who should take a spot-kick – Jones had been chosen. Jones was called to take the kick. He waved them away, as though saying: "In my state of health I cannot accept the joy of a penalty." Dodds arrived at the spot and Sidlow got a hand to the shot without quite getting it outside the bar, or over the top.

'Ah, yes, this game poor in its first stanza had drama in its second, and in its final stages it made a perfect sample of Liverpool football. No-one should complain of the result or of the play. Everton directors were faced outside their entrance door by a tract reading: "How can ye escape?"

'But these directors slept peacefully on Saturday night because the call-up of "1930 and all that" had consolidated the side into a working party with direction and a lot of wise passing and cajolery by Stevenson (capt), all the half-backs and others.

'Everton were at least playing football, a novelty this season. Where their home spectators had been concerned there was now a complacent thought that, after all, the home firm isn't really so bad. I warn selectors that the older generation cannot expect to tread light fantastic steps when grounds become holding.

'At this stage I want to bring readers to the excellence of most of Liverpool's work and the fact that they probably feel they could and should have won. They got the opening goal – they could have had more, but for two concrete reasons. I have never seen a more electrifying save than that which foiled the best shooter of both sides – Fagan.

'Payne cross-headed the ball and Fagan, without endeavouring to trap or stem the flow of the ball, struck it instantaneously, the effect being that there was ferocious pace on the ball.

'It was such a diversion of normality in football angles that Sagar had no right to make a save and that fact makes his arrest of the ball at the foot of the upright the most startling save of his life – excelling his cut-out of the Liddell in-swinger.

'Fortunately Fagan was able to take a goal and he appeared to stand petrified when he had scored via the upright.

'The making of this goal was due to excellent pairing by Shannon and Payne, babes in football arms, who interchanged positions on the right wing, Liddell's effort rebounding to Fagan's feet.

'There is so much to tell, so little space in which to do everyone justice. I must put in evidence the superiority of Liverpool for three parts of the play and their constant shooting as compared with Everton, crashing on a splendid trio in Jones, Taylor (three-star) and Paisley, and Liverpool's backs in resolute form.

'Payne was perky and inclined to ignore the wise, bald pate of Balmer (he hit the woodwork and continues to be luckless in his best efforts this season), who called for a cross at Payne's convenience, whereas Payne travelled in and around, scissoring his legs over the ball like a Tisky and making his task a little more difficult than it need have been.

'Payne, wonderful prospect, must not overdo it.

'A word to the stalwart and striking Shepherd, who looks a McKinley in embryo. Boyes picked up the ball and handed it to a Liverpool player for a throw-in. That was sportsmanship and gained him applause for a very simple manliness where often stupidity arises over these trifles. Shepherd (and this does not apply to his penalty incident) did something one will not allow in Derby or other games.

'A refreshing game, a fascinating game, moderate in quality till the later stages, but always having interest. Now if Liddell had not "pressed" he could have pressed home Liverpool's advantage. His impetuous intense shooting is born of enthusiasm, but lacks the timing necessary to keep a straight path.

'Well done all, especially the gallant old gentlemen of the 30s.'

MATCH STATS

EVERTON: Sagar, Saunders, Hedley, Bentham, Jones, Watson, Powell, Fielding, Dodds, Stevenson, Boyes.

LIVERPOOL: Sidlow, Shepherd, Lambert, Taylor, Jones, Paisley, Payne, Balmer, Shannon, Fagan, Liddell.

GOALS: EVERTON Dodds (84 pen)
LIVERPOOL Fagan (80)
ATTENDANCE 78,299

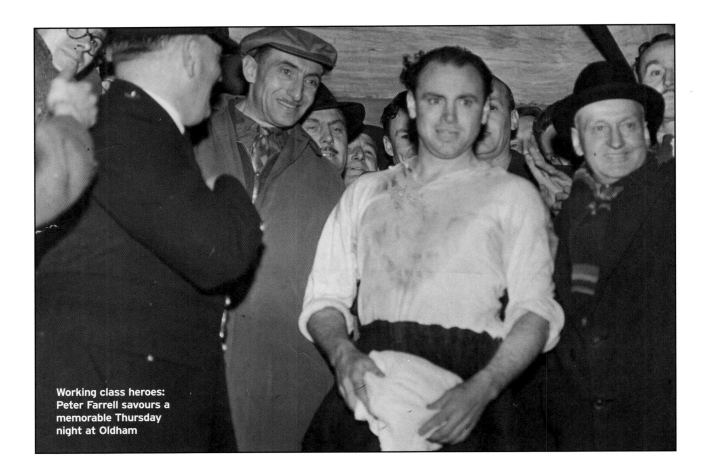

Working class heroes:
Peter Farrell savours a
memorable Thursday
night at Oldham

'Thousands swarmed on to the pitch and hoisted Farrell shoulder high'

IN August 2002, Everton became the first team in English football to celebrate 100 years of top-flight football.

But while modern soccer stars like Wayne Rooney, Thomas Gravesen and Kevin Campbell basked in that achievement, the unique record had much to do with a group of more working-class heroes who had graced Goodison Park 48 years earlier.

On a Thursday night in Oldham – on April 29, 1954 – Everton ended a brief exile in a lower level of English football for the last time.

Idols like Dave Hickson, John Willie Parker and Peter Farrell were roared on by a huge travelling army of Evertonians. A 4-0 victory at Oldham Athletic, who were relegated to Division Three North, ensured Everton were promoted back into the top flight after a three-year absence.

Peter Farrell, the captain who led the side when they dropped out of the First Division in 1951, also led them back. The fans showed their appreciation as they chaired him off the Boundary Park pitch.

More than 20,000 Evertonians had made the journey into the Lancashire hills – and a few had even gathered at midnight outside Goodison Park to welcome the team back home again.

A famous occasion was captured by the *Echo's* correspondent of the day, "Ranger".

FIRST HALF GOAL RUSH –
AND EVERTON ARE THERE
Tough exchanges mar later stages of game

By Ranger

'By defeating Oldham Athletic 4-0 at Boundary Park last night, Everton brought about the desired culmination of their long drawn-out struggle this season for promotion to the First Division of the Football League.

'Everton were infinitely the better side in the first half

and established a lead of three goals at the end of 26 minutes, partly due to two lapses by Burnett, the former Everton goalkeeper who captained Oldham for the occasion. A fourth goal, 10 minutes later, made the issue clear.

'At the halfway stage it looked quite on the cards that Everton might win by a sufficiently large margin to overhaul Leicester City as champions. In the second half, however, the game was marred by much rough play and many exhibitions of ill temper.

'The Everton players were occasionally stung to retaliation and the referee, in turn, spoke to Hardwick, Smith, Hickson and Moore, while even the usually equable-tempered Eglington was involved in one incident after a particularly aggravating foul.

'There were scenes of tremendous enthusiasm as soon as the final whistle went. Everton's supporters, who had gone to Oldham by road and rail in a steady stream throughout the day to the extent it is estimated of somewhat in the vicinity of 20,000, let themselves go deliriously.

'Thousands of them swarmed onto the playing pitch and hoisted Farrell, the Everton captain, shoulder high, carrying him in triumph to the entrance of the dressing room. The jubilant and excited spectators refused to disperse until the players had shown themselves and kept chanting "We want Peter" until Farrell came to the front again to acknowledge their cheers.

'Everton have thus preserved First Division football for Merseyside next season. The City of Liverpool has never been without a club in the top flight of all since the Football League was formed in 1888.

'The Goodison club achieved their ambition to recapture senior status after three years in the lower sphere. The players will be assured of a tremendous welcome when the Liverpool Senior Cup final with Liverpool takes place next week, although nothing could excel in fervour and jubilation the demonstration which was given them at the close of this Boundary Park game.

'It was Parker who set Everton on the road to victory when he gave them the lead in the seventh

BACK WHERE WE BELONG

OLDHAM ATH 0, EVERTON 4
Second Division, April 29, 1954

Report by 'Ranger'

minute after Moore had centred the ball from long distance and Hickson had headed it forward. Parker took advantage of a partial slip by the Oldham defence to nip in quickly and head it home for his 30th league goal of the season.

'Eglington missed a good chance of putting Everton further ahead in the 13th minute but a second goal was not long delayed.

'When it came it was due again to a defensive error, this time Burnett being at fault when he advanced too far to take command of a long shot by Jones, who was actually in the Everton half, just inside the centre circle, when he took this very tentative shot at goal.

'Burnett, however, strongly challenged by Hickson, allowed the ball to drop behind him into the net as he endeavoured to palm it out with one hand.

'This goal came at the 18th minute, and Oldham up to this time had not put in a solitary shot. Everton were playing beautiful football, keeping the ball on the ground and finding their men with unerring accuracy. A shot by Fielding struck Naylor and almost beat Burnett, who was fortunate to be able to turn the ball round and fall on the ball as it seemed certain to roll over the line.

'Hickson netted in the 23rd minute but the referee, after pointing to the centre, disallowed the point for a foul on Burnett and awarded a free-kick to Oldham.

'Parker scored a third for Everton at 26 minutes after Burnett had dropped

Great goal: Dave Hickson

On target: John Willie Parker

Fielding's shot and Parker, following up quickly, turned the ball into goal.

'The game was now as good as won, and it was then that one's thoughts turned to the possibility of Everton overtaking Leicester City on goal average and winning the Championship. This hope was encouraged when, at the 36th minute, Parker cleared the ball from the edge of the Everton penalty area, where he had been helping the defence in one of Oldham's spasmodic raids, and Hickson, after running half the length of the field and beating three men, scored Everton's fourth goal with a left-foot drive out of Burnett's reach. This was a great individual effort and the best goal of the evening.

'Hickson was on the receiving end of some vigorous treatment by the home defence and in the closing stages of this half, Oldham began to show some improvement on their earlier ineffective and disappointing display.

'After the entrancing football which Everton had served up in the first half, the second portion was something of an anti-climax. The visitors appeared to slacken off considerably in their efforts and allowed Oldham to take the upper hand for quite lengthy spells.

'It was 15 minutes before Everton tried a shot in the second half, during which time O'Neill had twice saved brilliantly from Harris. Harris also went close a third time with a header which missed the post by inches.

'Hickson twice worked his way through only to be foiled by Burnett. Eglington also missed by inches with an oblique header following a free-kick by Jones. The longer the second half progressed the more did the game deteriorate from an exhibition of football into something which at times took on the aspect of a brawl.

'The referee spoke to several players in turn. At one period, after an incident between Hardwick and Moore, pieces of bread and a bottle were thrown on to the playing pitch. Later, when Hickson was brought down by Naylor, Eglington adopted a threatening attitude, which is something entirely foreign to his normal nature. Everton, however, despite the grim determination and forceful tactics of Oldham, defended cleverly and the covering of Jones, Donovan and Moore was first class.

'The visitors had to struggle for most of the second half, with Wainwright a limping passenger at outside right. Had the game pursued the same even tenor as in the first half, Everton would probably have increased their lead, but in the face of Oldham's rugged tactics, plus a spot of retaliation on the part of one or two of their own players, the rhythm and precision went out of the side.

'Nevertheless, it was an excellent victory, much to the liking of the vast crowd of supporters and though the Goodison club have to be satisfied with second place to Leicester, that is a minor detail in comparison with the fact that promotion has at last been achieved.

'All the players on the Everton side did their part nobly in this victory, with the defence excellent throughout and the forward line showing style and artistry in the first half which emphasised the vast difference between a prospective First Division side and one which is doomed to return to the Northern section.

'Hardwick, who led Oldham's attack in the first half, changed places with Brierley during the second half. Naylor was Oldham's best defender.

'The official attendance was 40,000.'

MATCH STATS

OLDHAM ATHLETIC: Burnett, Smith, McGlen, Lowrie, Naylor, White, Walker, Harris, Hardwick, McLivenny, Brierley.

EVERTON: O'Neill, Moore, Donovan, Farrell, Jones, Lello, Wainwright, Fielding, Hickson, Parker, Eglington.

GOALS: EVERTON Parker (7, 26), Jones (18), Hickson (36)
ATTENDANCE 40,000 (30,072 in record books)

'Hickson, after running half the length of the field and beating three men, scored Everton's fourth goal with a left-foot drive'

'If the Pier Head pigeons were disturbed by the noise, I would not be surprised'

JOHN Moores was the power behind the throne at Everton throughout a golden age in the club's history.

Chairman during the trophy-laden years of Harry Catterick's reign, Moores was the man who took the decision to sack Johnny Carey – in a London taxi – then brought Catterick to Goodison and backed his judgement in the transfer market with a string of big-money signings.

But the Moores and Catterick dream ticket might have split right from the start.

Everton were crowned League champions on a vibrant afternoon in May 1963 – and the *Echo's* Michael Charters revealed in his colourful match report that Moores had threatened to stand down if the title hadn't been landed that afternoon.

We'll never know how real Moores' threat was, because Everton demolished Fulham 4-1 to land their sixth league title.

Under the headline: **'VERNON MAKES IT V-DAY FOR EVERTON'**, Michael Charters wrote:

'Has there ever been an atmosphere, an excitement, a thrill sports-wise in Liverpool, to equal that at Goodison Park on Saturday?

'Old-timers who have seen the great football moments in this city over the past four decades say there has been nothing like it since Dixie Dean broke the goalscoring record in 1928 in the last match of the season on the same pitch.

'It was a privilege to be in the historic ground again, this time to see Everton win the Football League Championship by crushing Fulham 4-1 to the accompaniment of the roaring acclaim of 60,000 delirious fans. The occasion was made, of course, by the knowledge that victory for Everton made certain of the trophy and the fans roared with laughter when a loudspeaker announcement, in giving the results of the Tottenham and Leicester games, commented: "Now let's see who could be the runners-up."

'I give full marks to the man who made it; he captured the bubbling-over mood of the fans who had cheered their team to a first championship win since 1939.

'The players, the crowd, everybody entered into the carnival spirit when the game and the championship had been well and truly won. A massive ring of policemen prevented any wholesale surge onto the pitch by the supporters – apart from a dozen or so youngsters hotly pursued by the law – and the team were able to make their lap of honour as the huge crowd stood and cheered themselves hoarse.

'If the Pier Head pigeons were disturbed by the noise I would not be surprised. It was shattering, ear-shaking approval for the Everton team and management who had come through to the title with a magnificent home straight run, in which they had taken 20 out of the last 24 points at stake. Championship form, champagne for the players afterwards, and champagne football from the side, at least in the first half when the game was settled by taking a 3-1 lead.

Classy: Roy Vernon

'Not a soul moved out until the lap of honour was ceremoniously completed, and the on-pitch congratulations had been joyfully exchanged between team and supporters.

'Then the crowd turned their attention to the occupants of the directors' box, calling: "We want John Moores."

'The hatless chairman – he lost his hat when he threw it up after Everton's second goal – acknowledged their applause, and then the fans wanted to see the team again.

'They saw them, led by Roy Vernon, still in their playing strip, champagne bottles in hand, with Tony Kay doing a

'The crowd, 15 minutes from the end, could sense that it was all over and they set up their giant "Ev-er-ton" chant and continuous cheering which reached its peak when Vernon scored the fourth goal five minutes from the end to make absolutely sure Everton were tops in every sense'

Champions! Fans created an 'amazing atmosphere' as the players did a lap of honour

war dance of joy in front, smoking the biggest cigar I've seen outside the Winston Churchill type.

'The crowd loved it, and the only time they were quiet was to hear Vernon pay tribute to the supporters, the rest of the team and the management. It was a neat speech and expressed all that had to be said.

'It was one big, happy family – the sort of feeling one gets but rarely, and only sport can provide it on these truly great occasions. One felt that there was a mutual feeling of appreciation between the players and their supporters. On one side the satisfaction of a hard job well done and finished with a flourish; on the other, genuine acknowledgement of the team's performances over a long, hard grind of 42 tough matches which has brought them, among other features, the finest defensive record and the best away record in the League, and their 40th home League and Cup game without defeat.

'Everton won this match with a top-class exhibition in the first half. After the interval they played with the intent of "what we have, we hold" and the game became ordinary. But the crowd, 15 minutes from the end, could sense that it was all over and they set up their giant "Ev-er-ton" chant and continuous cheering which reached its peak when Vernon scored the fourth goal five minutes from the end to make absolutely sure Everton were tops in every sense.

'They were two-up after eight minutes, both goals coming from the accurate boot of Vernon, and really they sewed up the game there and then. All three goals were similar in build-up and pattern, a remarkable feature which would have made headlines on any other day but this. That the team captain should clinch the title with three goals provided another story-book point to a day right out of the realms of fiction.

'For his first goal, Vernon won possession of the ball on the edge of the penalty area from Mullery when it looked odds-on the Fulham wing-half taking control of Parker's long through pass.

'Vernon had it, however, and he sped on, drawing Macedo out of goal, beating him with his swerve and pace and slotting the ball down a narrow angle and into the net.

'The next goal also involved the same four players. Vernon chased Parker's clearance with Mullery in front of him and looking certain to be able to touch the ball back to Macedo. But Vernon worried Mullery into hitting the ball hard against the goalkeeper, it rebounded to him and he went on, drawing Macedo over to the right to score from practically the same spot as the first goal.

'Following two isolated thrusts from Fulham, in which Dunlop made a splendid save from Cook, and then was beaten by an accurate, if slowly-hit shot from outside-right Key, who received the ball after a delightful Haynes-Robson passing duet on the right. It was thus 2-1 but Everton were in the groove. Kay – a magnificent performance of class and power all through – and Gabriel

were coming up to join the attack and they were pounding the Fulham defence.

'Young, brilliant in his heading, distribution and artistry, was giving Keetch immense trouble, and with Stevens having one of his best games of the season (how good to hear the crowd applauding him after the nightmare of the previous Saturday), the Everton forwards were moving with skill and polish. Stevens had the ball in the net from another delightful headed pass by Young, but the referee had, a second before, blown for a foul by Keetch on Young.

'But all was well, for Everton scored their third goal from the free-kick. Vernon's initial shot rebounded off a Fulham player to Scott, whose low shot struck a Fulham man en route and was deflected just inside the upright.

'Only once after that did Fulham look like scoring, but Dunlop made a splendid save from Cook's header midway through the second half, which was something of an anti-climax after the thrills of the first, but Everton were never in danger of failing. They were always on top, even if their pace had slowed and the whole tempo of the game became more pedestrian.

'Vernon raised it to the heights again with the last goal of the season. Young headed the ball through, Vernon once again beat Mullery in a close challenge for the ball, drew Macedo out to the right of the goal, and then directed the ball through the narrow gap into the far corner of the net. It was all over, only the congratulations were to come.

'Fulham fought hard, cleanly and well. There were no weaknesses in the Everton side. All played their part 100 per cent, but I must single out Kay, Young, Vernon and Labone for special mention.

'After the players had changed they came up to the boardroom to join a happy party, where chairman John Moores and manager Harry Catterick had sore hands receiving the congratulations which they have justly earned for their part in the Everton success story. Mr

Moores revealed that he intended to vacate the chairmanship if they had not won the championship, but was prepared to stay on now. He would still have been a director prepared, as he said, to help financially whenever the club needed.

'He paid fulsome praise to Mr Catterick as a great manager, whose handling of the playing staff could not be faulted and thought the team would be even better next season. Winning the title was one of his great ambitions, but he would have been content to have seen them in the top three, as he said at the start of the season. The turning point in recent games, he thought, was the victory at West Ham, who had beaten them in the Cup and were a very strong side on their own ground.

'Asked if the club intended to buy again before next season, Mr Moores said that they were completely satisfied with the team naturally, but if someone became available whom the management thought would be an asset to them, they would make a move for him. At present, there was no player of the class Everton would want available in the country.

'He said the decision to spend £100,000 on the signings of Kay and Scott during the time of no football in the freeze-up had been completely justified. The team had been playing very well before Christmas to lead Division One, but it was felt when they had time to assess the situation during the bad weather that they could strengthen the side with these two players. Results had proved them right.

'Mr Catterick said he felt the team always had a chance of winning the title, and he also referred to the West Ham game as a turning point. He paid tribute to Tom Egglestone, the trainer who was with him during their successful years at Sheffield Wednesday, and also to the rest of the coaching staff.

'Mr Catterick, a cautious man loathe, quite rightly, to make forecasts, would make no predictions about next season with its high promise of European Cup football. All he would say was that it was a very tough competition in which to succeed. But he has, in the past, told me that he thought the team would be better next season than this.

'So all is set fair for Everton. With a great and triumphant season only just behind them, thoughts are cast ahead to more and greater success to come.'

MATCH STATS

EVERTON: Dunlop, Parker, Meagan, Gabriel, Labone, Kay, Scott, Stevens, Young, Vernon, Temple.

FULHAM: Macedo, Cohen, Langley, Mullery, Keetch, Robson, Key, Brown, Cook, Haynes, O'Donnell.

**GOALS: EVERTON Vernon (5, 8, 83), Scott (27)
FULHAM Key (19)
ATTENDANCE 60,578**

Tony Kay in away action, and (below) the victorious 1963 title-winners. Opposite page: An excited fan is dealt with by the police

'Twice Labone said to me: 'Pinch me Jack, just so that I know it's true"

The toss: Everton skipper Brian Labone looks to see who has won the right to kick off the 1966 FA Cup final

BY the time the 1960s were in full swing, pen names like "Bee" and "Stork" had been consigned to the archives. Journalists used their own names and were encouraged to offer their own opinions.

The *Daily Post's* Jack Rowe was more than happy to oblige – and after the FA Cup final of 1966, he had plenty to comment upon.

The headline read: **'FINEST FIGHTBACK IN THE HISTORY OF WEMBLEY'.**

And Jack Rowe made it perfectly clear how highly he rated Everton's achievement.

'Don't let anyone try and kid you that this was the finest Cup final fightback, the finest recovery, rally or whatever word they use, since Stanley Matthews took Blackpool by the scruff of the neck and hauled them to that historic Wembley victory over Bolton Wanderers in 1953. Nobody is going to kid me about that anyway, because I put what happened at Wembley on Saturday even higher than 1953.

'My experience at Wembley finals may be limited in terms of years, but it goes back quite a bit and my recollections and my praise for what Matthews did in

1953 take second place to none.

'Yet I put Everton's triumph above that for two simple reasons. Bolton, if you remember, were handicapped by an injury to Bell and even if you are leading by two goals, in such a situation, with a man like Matthews on the opposing side anything is likely to happen and it did.

'But for me it was all so different on Saturday. Wednesday had grabbed their two goals. They were riding as high as any team possibly could be and Everton, with a bare 29 minutes to play, looked down and out.

'There were no injuries in the Wednesday ranks and, let's be frank, there was no Matthews on the other side either.

'What then, enabled Everton to literally drag themselves up off the deck and in 14 of the most dramatic, exciting and stupendous minutes deliver the most historic knockout blow ever seen at Wembley?

'The answer for my money, anyway, came in the dressing room afterwards and the man who delivered it was Brian Labone, the Everton captain.

'Labone has never walked around in a dream on or off the field, but he was near to it when he came down the tunnel with the Cup in his hands.

'Twice he said to me: "Pinch me Jack, just so that I know it's true." I obliged and he knew it was true all right and after the second occasion he said: "Team spirit did it, nothing else. This is the team a lot of people have been saying were all individuals, who had no spirit to fight.

'"Perhaps this will convince everybody that we have team spirit. I know it looked a bit bad out there when we were two-down and I won't pretend that I wasn't a bit worried, but I thought that if we could get a quick goal we must have a chance.

'"Well, Mike Trebilcock got the quick goal and from that moment we were inspired."

'I don't think there is a better description of why Everton won than that. No team without great spirit could have fought back like they did, no team without great spirit could have kept going as they did under the two Wednesday hammer blows and on a pitch which was so stamina sapping.

'Jimmy Gabriel said they had to drag their studs from the clinging grass almost every time they took a stride and when you have to face this sort of effort on top of a two-goal deficit at Wembley, it needs something out of the ordinary to do what Everton did.

'I thought also that in the finish Everton had the little extra experience and skill which helped them to make the spirit count and never was this better illustrated than when Derek Temple scored the goal in the 73rd minute which brought the Cup to Goodison Park and gave Merseyside the fabulous double.

'Gerry Young, the Wednesday half-back, erred, I know, when he tried to trap Colin Harvey's long forward lob and the ball ran away from him, but there was only a split second for Temple to size up the situation.

'He was on to it like a flash and as he moved forward towards the outcoming Springett, I swear that the whole of Wembley held its breath.

'What would Temple do? There they were face to face, two men with a wealth of experience between them and one of them, Springett, one of the best goalkeepers to wear an England jersey. To me, the odds were on Springett because he could narrow the shooting space and probably make Temple hurry his effort as he saw the goalkeeper coming out.

'Here again the player can tell you himself, because he alone knew what was in his mind as he came up against the moment of truth, because it was a moment of truth for Temple.

'Said Derek afterwards: "When I saw Springett coming out I was going to try and chip the ball over him, but he stopped on the six-yard line.

'"Then I was torn between taking the ball up to him and trying to dribble past him or hitting it.

'"I decided to hit it and it paid off, but I wouldn't like to be in that position again at Wembley, unless of course the same thing happened."

'Temple, you see, did not panic. His experience kept

THE GREATEST CUP FINAL COMEBACK

EVERTON 3, SHEFFIELD WEDNESDAY 2
FA Cup final, May 14, 1966

Report by Jack Rowe

For he's a jolly good fellow: Blues boss Harry Catterick is held aloft during the lap of honour

him steady at a time of crisis and his shooting skill enabled him to deliver a ball which would have beaten any goalkeeper anywhere.

'I rate this the best goal of the five because it had to be taken calmly and without blemish because if Temple had missed he would have gone into the Wembley story in a vastly different way than he will now.

'I am not forgetting by any means the two goals Mike Trebilcock, the young man who came into the Everton side for Fred Pickering and also wrote his name into the book of fame, scored.

'They were great ones and it seems fantastic that out of the three he has scored for Everton since he came from Plymouth Argyle, two should be on the occasion which is the greatest in the life of a player.

'His first, in the 59th minute, was the better of the two in my view because here he was in a similar sort of situation which faced Temple, although any criticism had he failed would not have reached the volume which would have gone in Temple's direction.

'It was Harvey again who put the ball forward and this time it was Temple who flicked it down with his head, smack in front of the in-running Trebilcock.

'Trebilcock struck it first time and Springett was left groping as the ball whizzed into the bottom corner of the net, wide of his left hand.

'When I asked Trebilcock later if he had tried to pick his spot, his reply was: "Not really. All I wanted to do was to keep it low because it's so easy to get under it. I knew if I

did keep it low it must have a chance of going in."

'The equaliser, five minutes later, came when Everton were awarded a free-kick not far outside the penalty area. Scott took it and chipped the ball to the far side when Labone challenged two Wednesday defenders.

'Some thought that Labone actually made the contact and misheaded the ball backwards, where Trebilcock met it some 15 yards out and with a right-foot swerving shot taken on the half volley again left Springett groping in anguish.

'But Labone did not touch the ball. His description was: "I went up but did not get to it and landed flat on my back. The next thing I heard was the swish of the ball in the net. What a lovely sound that was."

'Wednesday's goals, by comparison, were nothing like as clearcut, but they were worth the one they led with at half-time scored by McCalliog in the fourth minute.

'The centre-forward swept a cross from Quinn goalwards with his left foot and as West moved for it the ball struck Ray Wilson and was deflected to a spot which gave the Everton goalkeeper no hope of recovering.

'All the first half it was Wednesday who looked quicker to the ball and were the crisper in their passing action.

'To me Everton did not get into it at all, although I felt they were entitled to a penalty when Young was pulled down by Springett after he had taken the ball round the goalkeeper.

'Some of Gabriel's tackling in the first half was more lunging than practical and when the teams went off at half-time one was left with the feeling that Everton were not going to find anything like a rhythm or a purpose.

'But at least they never tried to shut the game up and with Wednesday playing as well as they were, it was all so entertaining and the Yorkshire side did their full part in making it a final worth watching.

'The second goal, and the one everybody thought was going to be the killer, was scored by Ford in 57 minutes, but Everton contended that Harris was pulled back before Fantham took the ball inside the penalty area and then drove in powerfully.

'West was in line for it alright, but could not keep a grip and as it rebounded Ford rushed in and pushed the ball just inside the post.

'I sensed the wilting in the mass of Everton fans behind the goal where it was scored and I certainly don't blame the Sheffield photographer deciding to get his colour camera ready for the presentation while his Liverpool colleague, *Daily Post* cameraman Neville Willasey, took the view: "Well, I won't need it now."

'We know who needed it in the end and the result is the picture you see today, but at that moment Everton were on their knees and I am convinced they would not

'I saw Harris in the dressing room sitting contentedly with a bottle of milk in his hand. For him the occasion must have almost been too much' have won if Trebilcock had not scored as quickly as he did.

'They simply had to get a quick goal because as Ray Wilson said, the longer you go without a score when you are down and struggling, the burden becomes greater and greater.

'The goal came, fortunately, and Gabriel's attitude was: "It seemed to bring us to life. We started clicking and stepped up the pace."

'He was right and in those 14 minutes we saw a transformation which I did not believe possible. There is no doubt that Everton finished the stronger because Wednesday had probably given all they had in building up the two-goals lead.

'But like Everton, they too never gave up and right to the final whistle sought to retrieve a situation which had been whipped from their grasp.

'Actually they should have been beaten 4-2 because Trebilcock failed with the game's best opening when Young slid the ball in front of him, but one of the day's heroes did the opposite to what Temple had done and tried to dribble round Springett instead of shooting quickly and lost it.

'It didn't matter in the end because every Everton player lifted himself up when the chips were down and as far as I am concerned it was a team which won the Cup, a team led by a fine captain in Brian Labone and one which had rewritten the Goodison Park story this season.

'Wembley 1966 will be full of happy memories for them all and they are entitled to them. I am delighted they won and if I mention Labone, Brian Harris and Temple in particular it is because they have been with the club so long.

'I saw Harris in the dressing room sitting contentedly with a bottle of milk in his hand. For him the occasion must almost have been too much.

'He knows that he has not much further to go in a top-class football career which has already spanned more than ten years and a winners medal will be something to treasure. I'm glad he's got it because the service he has rendered to Everton has been magnificent. Brian had two ambitions, to get to Wembley and win the Cup. They've come true. Everton manager Harry Catterick was one of the first to go into the Wednesday dressing room when it was all over.

'To win the League and Cup in four seasons is its own triumph for him and trainer Tommy Egglestone and they have the knowledge that the team paid its own tribute to them by the way they fought and won.

'Wednesday were disappointed as losing men at Wembley always must be and nothing anyone can say will be any consolation, but they put up a great show and Eustace, Fantham and Quinn were as good as any player on the pitch.

'They will never be able to understand how they lost what looked to be an unassailable position, but I shall remember their contribution to a fine final with gratitude.'

MATCH STATS

EVERTON: West, Wright, Wilson, Gabriel, Labone, Harris, Scott, Trebilcock, Young, Harvey, Temple.

SHEFFIELD WEDNESDAY: Springett, Smith, Megson, Eustace, Ellis, Young, Pugh, Fantham, McCalliog, Ford, Quinn.

GOALS: EVERTON Trebilcock (59, 64), Temple (73)
SHEFFIELD WEDNESDAY McCalliog (5), Ford (57)
ATTENDANCE: 100,000

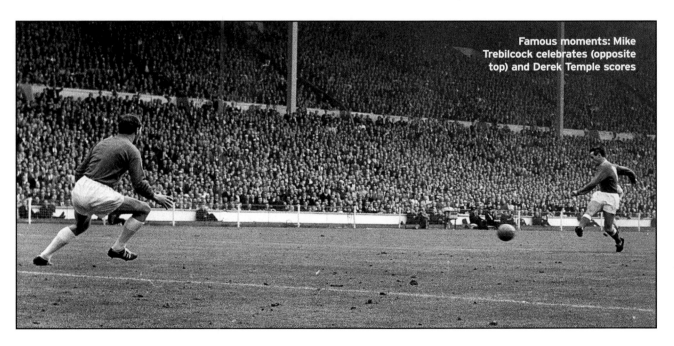

Famous moments: Mike Trebilcock celebrates (opposite top) and Derek Temple scores

Eddie's famous Wembley dash

EDDIE CAVANAGH has been labelled football's first hooligan. But such a moniker is both unfair and inaccurate.

Eddie's famous dash across the Wembley turf in 1966 wasn't borne of a desire to disrupt or attention seek, it was an instinctive, joyous reaction to the ecstasy of seeing his team salvage a seemingly hopeless situation in an FA Cup final. Eddie, from Huyton, had actually been on Everton's books as a youngster. So when he raced onto the turf, shedding his jacket to elude the pursuing policemen, many of the players recognized him.

Brian Labone and Gordon West gathered around the arresting officers when they finally halted Eddie's 60 yard celebration, to plead for leniency, while Brian Harris famously put on the policeman's helmet which had come flying off. Even then, however, Eddie still managed to express his joy, swinging a rattle manically as four bobbies carried him off like a human stretcher!

Everton had just retrieved a two-goal deficit to equalize, and even though Eddie was ejected from the stadium, he was back on the terraces in time for Derek Temple's winning goal. It was a pitch invasion which captured the imagination of the country – and Eddie spoke about it in 1988, to the authors of *Three Sides of the Mersey*.

'When it come back to 2-2 that was something else, wasn't it? I'd seen Trebilcock and I went for him first. Well, he didn't know me, but I grabbed him, pulled him on the ground. Then I was going to go to Westy. I was going to say "Gordon, for God's sake don't let no more in, we'll get that now."

'I seen this bizzy come up to me and he caught up with me and got me by the coat, but I just took it off, stood off, but I didn't see the other fellow come round me. I'll tell you his name to this day – Edward Anthony New. He wasn't even a bizzy, he was only a special, but I didn't see him coming because he wouldn't have caught me.

'He got me down. I just put my hands back and I think about six of them had me pinned down like I was one of the train robbers. There was a big Sergeant with a stick in his hand – I'll never forget that bugger.

'"What shall we do Sarge?" He said. "Put him out."

'"We could put him back in the crowd." He said: "Put him out." I said: "Please your self, it's 2-2 now."

'When Everton actually won the Cup I was hysterical. A St John Ambulance man had me sitting on a stool, giving me water. If you love your side, like I do, you're not worried about your kids, or your Ma or Da, you're just wanting to win that Cup.'

'They clinched the title to a non-stop roar of chants... 'Ev-er-ton!''

TRUE Blue Evertonians – on the pitch and off it – are all too aware of the special atmosphere night matches at Goodison Park generate.

Whether it's the floodlights, a sense of anticipation growing all day, or just the extra time fans can spend in the pub after finishing work – there's always something special about evening kick-offs. But one night match, in particular, proved to be more captivating than most.

Michael Charters, the *Liverpool Echo* journalist who was present when the title was clinched in 1963, was inside the stadium again seven years later when Everton claimed their seventh league success. And this time Charters was adamant the atmosphere eclipsed anything he had witnessed inside Goodison before.

He related the scene in glowing terms, before going on to pen a more traditional report about Everton's 2-0 triumph over West Bromwich Albion.

'WHAT A NIGHT! WHAT AN EMOTIONAL, JOYOUS, CAPTIVATING NIGHT!'

'There was only one place to be in Liverpool last night and that was Goodison Park. The lucky ones were the 58,523 spectators (biggest crowd of the season) who were there to see Everton win the seventh League Championship in their history, their second in seven years...and win it with impressive authority and superb football.

'The result – a 2-0 win over West Bromwich – was never in doubt because of Everton's total command of the play. And this helped to ease any possible strain from the fans, who created an atmosphere of happy anticipation and adulation for their team much greater than seven years ago.

'It was not only the Gwladys Street fans who roared their team on in triumph. This was total, unreserved acclaim of the champions from every section of the crowd.

'Everton sparkled in their play to the sparkle of their fans' applause. They clinched the title to a non-stop roar of chants including "Ev-er-ton," "We are the champions," "We're on our way to Europe," "Send our team to Mexico" and even a couple of choruses of "When you're smiling."

'And one of the greatest roars of the night came during half-time when it was announced that manager Harry Catterick, watching with pride and joy the team he has built as it displayed football of high quality, had won the Manager of the Month award for March – the second time he has received it this season.

Glory again: Colin Harvey's 25-yarder clinches the championship on an unforgettable night

'Poor Albion: they could have been excused for wilting in an atmosphere of such emotion. This was Everton's night and they were there, indeed just to make up the numbers.

'The crowd awarded every throw-in, every corner, every free-kick, before referee Leo Callaghan could blow his whistle. They took over Goodison completely.

'And when it was all over – and how the players heard the final whistle midst such a din I'll never know – Harry Catterick was first on the pitch to greet his boys, throwing his arms around each one as they went off for a couple of minutes.

'Back they came for a lap of honour. And how good it was to see skipper Brian Labone, who missed the climax to the title through injury, take his place with the others.

'The fans gave him their special ovation as they chanted every player's name in turn.

'The lap of honour began with decorum, but ended in a wild display of enthusiasm as hundreds of fans spilled on to the pitch despite appeals to keep off.

'Then came the touch which completed this wonderful night. Mr Louis Edwards, chairman of Manchester United and a member of the League Management committee, was there to present the trophy which had been collected in secret from Leeds a couple of days ago.

'The players appeared in the directors' box one by one, each to be greeted with individual roars of acclamation. Alan Ball, captain in Labone's absence, received the trophy from Mr Edwards, who also handed the players their medals.'

'CHAMPIONS...AND THEY PLAYED LIKE IT'

'Everton's performance against West Bromwich at Goodison last night was full of the brilliance which has established them as a superb footballing side, a side which plays the game with a skill and speed as fine as anything we have seen for many years.

'I consider them a better team than that which won the title seven years ago. The championship is harder to win these days, but Everton thrilled and entertained crowds up and down the country with football of the highest quality. It was fitting that they should delight their own deliriously happy fans in their last home game of the season with a title-clinching display which contained all the joys and delights of their skills in one smooth, effective package.

'One could only feel sorry for Albion – or indeed any team – which had to try and make a game of it in the emotion-charged atmosphere of Goodison last night. They were on a hiding to nothing and accepted their football lesson with the best of sportsmanship.

'They were lucky not to be beaten by more than two goals...Everton were unlucky that they did not settle the championship issue with a grand slam of goals.

'Osborne, in the Albion goal, had a magnificent match.

Happy days: The late Alan Ball and Brian Labone toast success

And it was a good job for his team that he was in such form. His handling was faultless and he was kept very busy.

'After a 15-minute spell of settling in, when they were clearly feeling the tension of the occasion, Everton moved into overdrive. Albion were never in the game with the slightest chance of creating a surprise; they never looked like scoring.

'Indeed, they were allowed very little of the ball at all. The slightest hesitation invited an Everton tackle and, inevitably, loss of possession. Everton's urgency was such that they looked twice as quick, twice as sharp, on and off the ball.

'Everton's complete domination stemmed, rightly, from the department which has been their greatest asset all season – the midfield trio. Ball, Harvey and Kendall were tremendous and they will be the backbone of a side which I expect to improve over the next few years.

'With total control in midfield, Everton set up a series of attacks which had Albion defending desperately for 90 per cent of the game.

'Morrissey ripped them to shreds with one of his finest displays of the season, Whittle strengthened his place as the new idol of the crowd. Royle played his full part.

'Behind them was a cast-iron defence in which Kenyon

CHAMPIONS IN STYLE

EVERTON 2, WEST BROM 0
First Division, April 1, 1970

Reports by Michael Charters

played a commanding role, Hurst was steady as a rock, Wright and Brown comfortably in control on the rare occasions Albion were able to stir out of defence.

'And West? Well he had only one save to make, from Cantello, and was as much a spectator as the 58,523 crowd, the biggest of the season.

'This was a complete team triumph, a suitable climax to a season which began brilliantly, wavered a little in mid-season when the team was hit by injuries, and finished in the manner of a great championship outfit.

'Seven successive wins have confirmed that the title has been won utterly on merit...no team in history can have moved to a nine-point lead with such authority.

'The game itself was played to the background of a continuous roar of applause and acclamation from the fans. It was too one-sided to be a contest in the true sense of the word, but Everton's classical exhibition of flowing, accurate, speedy football could hardly have been bettered.

'They were as sharp as knives, and but for Osborne would have proved just as damaging in a scoring sense.

'They began with a top-pace thrust which almost brought Harvey a goal in the opening minutes, but Osborne made the first of his many fine saves by turning the ball over the bar.

'It was Whittle's goal after 20 minutes – his 11th in 14 league games – which really set them on the path of victory with joyous, exhibition football.

'When Harvey mishit an attempted shot from the edge of the area, Whittle gathered the ball under control and seemed to stand with it for ages – probably a couple of seconds – before unleashing a fierce shot which struck an Albion defender before hitting the roof of the net.

'Whittle has now scored in six successive games. Can there have been such a run by a 20-year-old when pressure of a title run has been so great?

'Osborne saved well from Morrissey's header, superbly from Wright's shot after the full-back had joined in the attacking fun and taken the ball 30 yards in a brilliant run.

'But the Albion keeper was beaten by Whittle's overhead kick which slid over the bar and a near miss by Royle, who deflected Whittle's pass onto the post.

'Kendall, always thrusting forward, hit two over the bar before Harvey settled it all midway through the second half with one of the great goals of the season.

'He collected the ball way out, took it down the left, turned back in his tracks and lost two of his shadowers at the same time, brought the ball into the middle and cracked a right-foot shot from 25 yards which left the airborne Osborne helpless.

'What a goal to clinch the title!

'That was it, of course. Royle headed against an upright but it didn't really matter.

'This was the style of champions, won in the truly grand manner.'

First goalscorer Alan Whittle receives the congratulations of boss Harry Catterick

MATCH STATS

EVERTON: West, Wright, Brown, Kendall, Kenyon, Harvey, Husband, Ball, Royle, Hurst, Morrissey.

WEST BROMWICH ALBION: Osborne, Hughes, Wilson, Fraser, Robertson, Merrick, Cantello, Suggett, Astle, Brown, Hope.

GOALS: EVERTON Whittle (20), Harvey (65)
ATTENDANCE 58,523

We're ready: Everton skipper Kevin Ratcliffe before kick-off

'It was an occasion to cherish, as rival fans shared a joke before the game'

AFTER 14 long years of trophy-free football at Goodison Park, Everton's FA Cup success in 1984 was riotously celebrated by relieved Evertonians. But for boss Howard Kendall, the FA Cup triumph was seen as a stepping stone to greater glories.

While Evertonians celebrated, he was already plotting future glories – and he expressed his thoughts in an exclusive interview in the *Liverpool Echo* on the Monday after Watford had been beaten 2-0 at Wembley Stadium.

Ian Hargraves reported:

'After the euphoria of Everton's FA Cup victory and their triumphant return home, manager Howard Kendall got down to business again today.

'His declared intention is to ensure that Wembley becomes a launching pad for the championship, rather than just the climax of an exciting season, and to do that he knows he must keep his team together and hopefully strengthen it.

'Tomorrow he welcomes new signing Paul Bracewell to Goodison as his first reinforcement and throughout the week, he will be trying to persuade four of his present squad to sign new contracts.

'"We will do everything we can to ensure that the players who have done so well for us this season remain with us," he told me today.

KENDALL'S CUP KINGS

EVERTON 2, WATFORD 0
FA Cup final, May 19, 1984

Reports by Ken Rogers

'"I know the fans want that and I am hopeful we shall be able to reach agreement all round. We want to build for the future so that the 1984 Cup starts the ball rolling for the championship, just as the 1968 final set the ball rolling for our title success two years later.

'"To win the FA Cup is fantastic, but in the long run it is the championship, achieved over 42 games, that has to be the main objective. The Cup was the icing, now we want the cake."'

Neville Southall and Graeme Sharp parade the FA Cup, while (bottom) manager Howard Kendall meets the Duke of Kent during the pre-match presentations

Kendall's words were prophetic. The FA Cup success in 1984 was the prelude to the most successful season in Everton's history and Wembley became almost a second home throughout the 1980s.

Later to become *Liverpool Echo* sports editor, Ken Rogers was present at every success.

Reproduced here is his report of that historic 1984 triumph.

'What a day, what a season. Merseyside's Big Two stand supreme, the untouchables of English soccer.

'The League Championship, the Milk Cup, the FA Youth Cup and now the FA Cup itself...they are all ours.

'Liverpool can still add European glory to this stunning array of silverware, but for the moment their famous rivals Everton are basking proudly in the spotlight, winners again after 14 long years.

'Saturday's 2-0 victory over Watford saw Howard Kendall's blue and white army take Wembley by storm. It was an occasion to cherish, the friendly final when rival fans shared a laugh and a joke before the game, posed with each other for photographs and revelled in the atmosphere and excitement of a marvellous occasion.

'But Cup finals are all about winners and Everton's unshakeable determination to claim that elusive piece of silverware was to prove decisive. Watford boss Graham Taylor had talked about enjoying the match and being part of a great day.

'His rival Howard Kendall, a three-time Wembley loser, could only talk about winning. Goals from twin strikers Graeme Sharp and Andy Gray were to give the Blues' boss possibly his proudest-ever moment, surpassing even his achievement in helping to win the League Championship for Everton back in 1970.

'The Ball-Harvey-Kendall midfield trio was to become legendary at Goodison. Now the Kendall and Colin Harvey backroom link has proved just as potent. They both choked back the tears as Kevin Ratcliffe held aloft the FA Cup. A season for swinging fortunes had ended on an unforgettably high note.

'Even before a ball was kicked Everton knew that the biggest threat to their chances would come from the talented John Barnes. The young winger was to live up to his exciting reputation, shaking the Blues early in the game with his pace, strength and superb skill.

'It's a pleasure to watch Barnes in full flight, a player who can light up any match with his natural ability. The task of containing him fell to another impressive young player, Blues right-back Gary Stevens.

'He was to rise to the challenge magnificently and as Everton imposed themselves on their opponents, the fans were to salute the adventure of another bright talent – Trevor Steven.

'What a game he was to have, finally laying on the cross from the right that saw Gray kill off Watford with typical spring and strength after 51 minutes.

'From that point there could only be one result with Everton firmly in the driving seat and their opponents struggling to pick themselves up off the floor.

'Yet what a start Graham Taylor's side had made. Lee Sinnott was using his ability as a long throw specialist to good effect, aiming for the giant George Reilly.

'In the first minute a knock-on gave Barnes a close-range heading chance, Neville Southall making a fine save.

'Everton's response was a dangerous cross from Steven that was glanced wide by Sharp and a strong run and shot into the sidenetting from Kevin Richardson.

'It was an outstanding first half, Adrian Heath setting off on a twisting chase for goal before attempting a chipped shot that was deflected for a corner.

'Watford bounced back, the Barnes magic flickering as his body swerve took him away from both Gary Stevens and Derek Mountfield. He got in his shot on the edge of the box with Southall spreading himself, but it was Mountfield who recovered to block the effort.

'The pressure wasn't over for the Blues with Les Taylor arriving to hammer inches wide of the left-hand post. Both sides had created good opportunities and Peter Reid, Everton's Player of the Year with 11 man-of-the-match nominations in the *Echo* during the season, showed his strength to shake off Kenny Jackett before curling a tremendous effort wide of the upright.

'The momentum of the game and the vast number of scoring chances at both ends made this an intriguing and entertaining final. Everton began slowly, then stepped up a gear to live up to their billing as favourites.

'The decisive blow came after 38 minutes, Wembley erupting in a sea of blue and white as Sharp suddenly found himself with the space just inside the box to strike a brilliant opener.

'Gary Stevens had won a challenge with Barnes, the ball breaking forward for Sharp to control and lash his shot into the corner of the net with goalkeeper Steve Sherwood completely helpless.

'The fans roared their delight. Watford were forced to dig deep into their reserves of character and spirit, but six minutes into the second half it was effectively all over.

'Trevor Steven's skill took him past full-back Neil Price. The midfield man sent over a teasing cross that looked ripe for the keeper to hold, but Gray rose with power and suddenly the ball was in the back of the net.

'Watford, pushed by Bob Wilson later on *Match of the Day*, complained that Sharp's effort was offside and that Gray had fouled Sherwood for the second. But to suggest that this victory was anything but fully deserved is an insult to a memorable match.

'The headlines in the *Echo's* Wembley souvenir edition, sported in the many cars on the motorway, had already said it all for the Evertonians...We're Back!'

MATCH STATS

EVERTON: Southall, Stevens, Bailey, Ratcliffe, Mountfield, Reid, Steven, Heath, Sharp, Gray, Richardson. Sub not used: Harper.

WATFORD: Sherwood, Bardsley, Price (Atkinson), Taylor, Terry, Sinnott, Callaghan, Johnston, Reilly, Jackett, Barnes.

**GOALSCORERS: EVERTON Sharp (38), Gray (51)
ATTENDANCE: 100,000**

Graeme Sharp's snap-shot opens the scoring in the 1984 Cup final

MAN OF THE MATCH

'In weighing up the contenders for the Everton Man of the Match you have to look at the battling efforts of goal heroes Graeme Sharp and Andy Gray, the undoubted ability of goalkeeper Neville Southall and the midfield determination of Peter Reid and Kevin Richardson.

'But no-one would deny that two young players on the right flank played a key role in this triumph.

Full-back Gary Stevens fought a mighty battle with John Barnes, a performance that was to earn him a salute from England boss Bobby Robson.

'The vote was finally edged to Trevor Steven, whose adventure and skill caused Watford all kinds of problems and who is emerging as one of the most exciting prospects in the game.'

Liverpool Echo's
Ken Rogers

THE MAGIC OF MUNICH

EVERTON 3, BAYERN MUNICH 1
European Cup Winners' Cup
semi-final second leg,
April 24, 1985

By Ken Rogers

'The final whistle came with the Goodison fans roaring out a deafening salute'

BY common consent, it is the most famous night in Everton's entire history. If Dixie Dean's record-breaking 60th league goal was the most exhilarating afternoon Goodison Park has ever witnessed, the night famous German giants Bayern Munich were mauled in front of 49,000 ecstatic Evertonians is regarded as the most emotional evening in Everton history.

The date was April 24, 1985, the occasion the second leg of the European Cup Winners' Cup semi-final – and the *Liverpool Echo's* Ken Rogers was inside Goodison to witness it.

'Everton gave one of the greatest club sides in Europe a one-goal start last night – and then battered them into submission to power into their first European final.

'Goodison Park exploded as goals from Graeme Sharp, Andy Gray and Trevor Steven broke the hearts of Bayern Munich.

'The West German league leaders thought they had this Cup Winners' Cup semi-final in the bag when Dieter Hoeness squeezed them in front after 37 minutes.

'But Everton, inspired by 11 heroes on the pitch and 49,000 never-say-die supporters on the terraces, hit back with a vengeance to clinch a famous victory and a final place in Rotterdam against Rapid Vienna on May 15.

'The courage, determination and commitment that inspired this triumph was epitomised in the displays of Everton's three goalscorers.

'Sharp and Gray gave the Germans a pounding with as good a display of front-running as you will see. It was the very best of British in terms of bold and aggressive centre-forward play and the reward was a goal apiece in the second half, when Bayern were on the rack and on the run as the Blues seized control.

'If that wasn't enough, Steven brought the house down four minutes from time like some latter-day Bobby Charlton, racing clear and unleashing an unstoppable shot from the edge of the box that flew past Belgian international keeper Jean Marie Pfaff to make it 3-1.

'The final whistle came with the Goodison fans roaring out a deafening salute on a night when Merseyside had two teams to be proud of in Europe.

'Skipper Kevin Ratcliffe rushed across to throw his arms around his Welsh international team-mate, Neville Southall, and every player received a standing ovation as he moved down the tunnel.

'Last off was Gray, savouring every second of the excitement. He thrust his fists high into the air, and the final cheer must have rattled the Bayern dressing room door as the Germans reflected bitterly on a remarkable game.

'The first half was a full-blooded, no-holds barred affair

'The Scot kicked out wildly in retaliation, an unfortunate rush of blood that could have proved costly, but he escaped with a caution and Pflugler joined him in the book'

that bubbled like a volcano at times as the Munich outfit tried to stem the Everton charge.

'In Hans Pflugler they had a hit man who infuriated the home fans as he twice sent Sharp crashing and then turned his attentions to Gray.

'The Scot kicked out wildly in retaliation, an unfortunate rush of blood that could have proved costly, but he escaped with a caution and Pflugler joined him in the book.

'In terms of chances Everton had totally dominated the action and Steven should have broken the deadlock after four minutes, snatching at his close-range shot and screwing the ball wide.

'Bayern had managed just a single shot on target when they suddenly stunned the Blues with the kind of swift break that was always a nagging possibility.

'Golden boy Ludwig Kogl found himself in the clear, and although Southall blocked his shot on the edge of the box, Hoeness followed up to squeeze the ball home between two defenders on the line.

'Three minutes into the second half Everton hit back when Gray knocked on a Stevens long throw and Sharp pounced for his 29th goal of the season, a glancing header that set up a storming finish.

'Another Stevens throw had Bayern at sixes and sevens after 75 minutes, with Pfaff failing to hold the ball and seeming to be impeded by two of his own players on the line.

'Gray scooped the ball home first time, to send the fans wild with excitement.

'Steven turned the screw in the 86th minute, and you won't see a sweeter build-up or a more decisive piece of finishing. Sheedy started it with a superb through ball, Gray's boot flicking it on, beyond his marker Nachtweih, and Steven advanced to wipe out the Germans in style.'

MATCH STATS

EVERTON: Southall, Stevens, Van den Hauwe, Ratcliffe, Mountfield, Reid, Steven, Sharp, Gray, Bracewell, Sheedy.

BAYERN MUNICH: Pfaff, Dremmler, Willmer (Belerorzer), Eder (Rummenigge), Augenthaler, Lerby, Pflugler, Matthaus, Hoeness, Nachtweih, Kogl.

GOALS: EVERTON Sharp (48), Gray (75), Steven (86)
BAYERN MUNICH Hoeness (37)
ATTENDANCE 49,476

Andy Gray and Graeme Sharp
celebrate with the Gwladys Street

MAN OF THE MATCH

'It is difficult to name a Man of the Match when a team has 11 heroes, but on a night when Everton had to show all their fighting qualities to move through to the final, Andy Gray and Graeme Sharp had to be major contenders.

'Trevor Steven's skill and pace also outshone German golden boy Ludwig Kogl, but the verdict went to Gray – a giant up front and the man who never let Bayern relax for a single moment.

'If you go and you haven't got a sore throat, you haven't done your job!'

EVERTONIAN ability to inspire their team to glory is renowned. But on one incredible afternoon in 1994, the power of the people was needed to support a much greater cause.

On May 7, 1994, Everton came as close as they had been in 40 years to losing their cherished top-flight place.

With a new stand at Goodison Park in the process of being constructed, stadium capacity had been slashed to 31,000 and one end of the ground stood empty.

But enterprising Evertonians came up with different ways to back the Blues in their hour of need. On the eve of the final match of the seson, the *Echo* carried the following story.

'An anxious Evertonian is urging fellow supporters to stand up for the club on Saturday – literally. Jim Plunkett, a Gwladys Street Ender who helped initiate the Goodison Derby scarf chain following the Hillsborough disaster, wants supporters to ignore their seats against Wimbledon and stand up for the full 90 minutes. He believes this will encourage the supporters to get behind the team more in a match Everton must win to save their Premiership skins.

'"Myself and a group of Everton fans are asking every Evertonian who goes to the ground on Saturday to stand up for the full 90 minutes, and shout and shout," he said. "It's embarrassing to have to do this, but we have to do something.

'"We've all heard it said so many times how much a crowd can lift a team and we want our supporters to do it."

'Other ideas Plunkett would like to implement in time for Saturday's big showdown include: taking loud hailers into the ground to urge supporters who are slacking to turn up the volume, leafletting outside the ground to urge fans to back the side and the introduction of cheer leaders.

'"We also want to send a delegation to meet Mike Walker for half-an-hour to ask for encouragement from the players," Plunkett added.

'"When they run out we don't just want to juggle with the ball for five minutes.

'"We want them to encourage us and get the crowd going. Our message is: 'If you go on Saturday and haven't got a sore throat, you haven't done your job.'"'

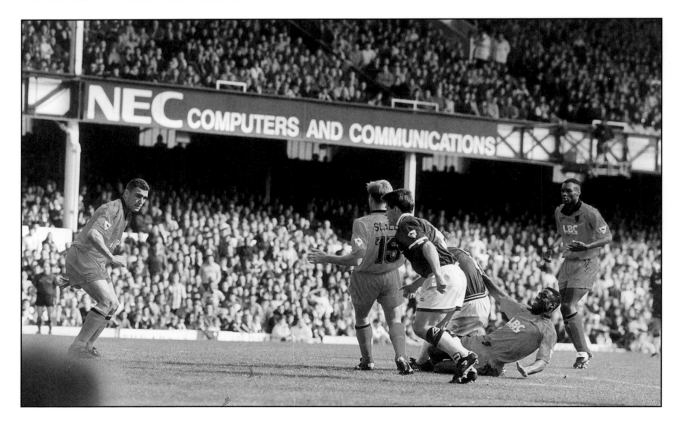

Days later, it became totally apparent that Evertonians had, indeed, done their job.

The *Liverpool Echo's* Everton correspondent, David Prentice, reported on an amazing Goodison occasion.

'It was heart-stopping and intensely exciting; it was raw, rich theatre. But after the dust had settled and the hangovers healed on one of the most amazing matches in Everton's history, there are just two words to be said to the incoming Goodison hierarchy: Never again.

'The Evertonian who lurched into the Winslow Hotel on Goodison Road with an inane grin stuck immovably onto his face, summed up Saturday sweetly. "How can Sheffield United go through that every season?" he queried. Everton went through the relegation shredder and survived – just – but it must never be allowed to get this close again.

'Peter Johnson's pre-match quotes on BBC Television were heartwarming. He wants to see changes both on and off the field at Goodison. He was there on Saturday to observe the enormous potential that still exists at this great club, but 12 months of boardroom banality have seen things sink to this pitifully low ebb.

'However, just when it mattered most, everybody pulled together.

'The support was sensational. Nostalgia lends past glories a greater glow than they possessed at the time, but I'm convinced Saturday's crowd volume was even greater than on that famous night nine years ago against Bayern Munich, even with one quarter of the ground missing.

'Two weeks ago Crystal Palace boss Alan Smith described Goodison Park as "a great stadium, but not exactly hostile." Wimbledon felt otherwise and Warren Barton's pre-match comments that he and his team-mates were concerned for their safety should they win were just the words Evertonians wanted to hear.

'The roar at kick-off made it impossible to be heard over the telephone by *Football Echo* copytakers – until three minutes past three. It was then that Anders Limpar had his "brainstorm" and needlessly handled Elkins' corner-kick. Dean Holdsworth just squeezed the spot-kick past Southall and the crowd was silenced.

'Everton's early play bore the stamp of blind panic, and Wimbledon's second goal was a defensive catastrophe. The admirable Davids, Watson and Unsworth, collided and Andy Clarke poked the ball wide of the Gwladys Street goal where Gary Ablett sliced it into his own net.

'It was time for heroes. Enter Graham Stuart and Barry Horne.

'Four weeks ago, when Stuart accepted the penalty-taking responsibility because no-one else, bar Southall, wanted it, he said: "I can just see it now. We'll get one in the last match against Wimbledon and I'll have to score to keep us up. I'll be terrified." Most Evertonians were unaware that Stuart had blasted his only other

THE GREAT ESCAPE

EVERTON 3, WIMBLEDON 2
FA Premier League, May 7, 1994

Report by David Prentice

spot-kick over a crossbar at Chelsea. This time he showed no nerves as he boldly converted.

'Then it was Horne's turn. Since the only meaningful second-half chances had been falling Wimbledon's way, the much-maligned midfielder snatched a bouncing ball off Jones' toes and headed for goal. Twenty-five yards out he unloaded an astonishing drive which curled wickedly into the top corner. "Who needs Cantona when we've got Barry Horne?" was the popular post-match chant.

'In contrast, the cruel joke afterwards was that Horne could become the first Evertonian to score his only goals for the club in his first and last matches. Whatever Horne's future, that single strike has already earned him cult hero status amongst the fans.

'Stuart, too, made his bid for legend with the goal that won the match nine minutes from time. Lunging right-footed at Cottee's knockback, Stuart spun the ball under Segers' dive where it nestled in the corner of the Gwladys Street net. Stuart's contributions in the last month have done as much as anybody to keep the Blues up.

'It was all about preserving Premiership status on Saturday - something that Evertonians have taken for granted for 40 years. Now that has been achieved, with Peter Johnson's ambition and sense of purpose, Bill Kenwright's enthusiasm and Mike Walker's vision, this must be the new beginning for the Blues. Saturday was wonderful, but never again...please.'

MATCH STATS

EVERTON: Southall, Snodin, Ablett, Unsworth, Watson, Ebbrell (Barlow), Stuart, Rideout, Cottee, Horne, Limpar.

WIMBLEDON: Segers, Barton, Elkins, Scales, Blackwell, Fear (Blissett), Jones, Earle, Gayle, Holdsworth Clarke.

GOALS: EVERTON Stuart (24 pen, 81), Horne (67) WIMBLEDON Holdsworth (4 pen) Ablett (20, o.g.) ATTENDANCE 31,297

'The support was sensational. Nostalgia lends past glories a greater glow than they possessed at the time, but I'm convinced Saturday's crowd volume was even greater than on that famous night nine years ago against Bayern Munich, even with one quarter of the ground missing'

'The roars for the new manager had barely subsided when there was a louder explosion'

DAVID MOYES had already captured the imagination of Evertonians on his first day as manager, with his "People's Club" catchphrase. But 24 hours later he showed he could back up his words with action.

Everton were flirting dangerously with the relegation zone in the Premiership when in-form Fulham came to Goodison Park in March 2002.

David Prentice reported on an afternoon when Evertonians rediscovered their pride in the People's Club.

'Optimism was the new buzzword at a bouncing Goodison Park on Saturday – and it gripped everybody.

'From Golden Goal timers to tartan talismans, a wave of enthusiasm washed over a stadium which had witnessed frustrated resignation just a fortnight earlier.

'The man with the stopwatch got so carried away he slashed five seconds off the time of the opening goal. David Unsworth's sugar-sweet strike was undeniably quick, but it was more 32 seconds than the 27 officially given out.

'Then there was Duncan Ferguson, winning headers, taking throw-ins, heading off his goalline and even chasing down goalkeeper's clearances.

'His performance was excellent and hugely influential. But gasps of admiration and nods of approval around the stadium were just as prevalent as disbelieving shakes of the head.

A NEW ERA

EVERTON 2, FULHAM 1
Premiership
March 16, 2002

Report by David Prentice

'It's a long time since we've seen Ferguson this committed, this driven and this exciting. Did it really take the arrival of a new manager and the psychological pick-me-up of the captain's armband to elicit such a reaction?

'Sadly the answer is in the affirmative. It will be a test of David Moyes' motivational skills to see if he can pluck other Braveheart performances like this one from the Scot's complex mind-set.

'But psychology is clearly a tool the new manager is adept at employing.

'When the roof almost came off Goodison Park at Graham Barber's final whistle, he swiftly blocked Ferguson's traditional early dart for the tunnel and sent him back out to join his team-mates and pay tribute to the outstanding support they had received.

'That crowd noise, as much as anything else, had helped Everton to the victory which was absolutely imperative to their Premiership survival hopes. And that is why Bill Kenwright's midweek gamble ultimately proved worth taking.

'Instead of an air of reluctant resignation around the stadium, there was enthusiasm. And when Everton were reduced to 10-men with more than an hour remaining, there was defiance, not fear.

'With minimal changes to the playing personnel – selected by coach Andy Holden – a new mood of optimism had swept Everton into a two-goal lead.

'But what the new regime hadn't banked on was the old indiscipline of Thomas Gravesen. If we were being kind you'd say Graham Barber flashes cards faster than Paul Daniels, and even less humorously. Seven yellow cards and a red was a harsh return from a committed but malice-free football match.

'But the fact remains that Gravesen committed a foul just about worthy of a caution, right under the fussy official's nose – just 17 minutes after collecting another undeniably deserved booking.

'That reduced Everton to 10 men, punctured the purposeful approach they had embraced from the off and introduced us to an hour of training ground attack against defence.

'It was an understandable reaction. Jean Tigana's Fulham pass the ball crisply, swiftly and imaginatively, but Everton refused to give them any holes to exploit.

'They sat back resiliently and resolutely, and just about ground out the result they required.

'It was an enervating afternoon. The roars which had greeted the new track-suited manager had barely subsided when David Unsworth sparked an even louder explosion of noise with a first-minute goal.

'Pistone's throw-in was won in the air by Ferguson, Radzinski touched the ball back to the only man operating out of position, note, and he caught hold of a sugar-sweet volley which ripped past Van der Sar.

'The same combination might have made it two in the 10th minute, but Radzinski's touch was poor this time and

he was forced to pass on responsibility to Unsworth, who fired just wide.

'But in the 12th minute we were confronted with a rare moment. Duncan Ferguson not only scored a Premiership goal from open play, he did so by unselfishly chasing down a goalkeeper's clearance.

'Two-nil up and a 34,639 crowd vibrant, the champagne corks were loosening, but when have Everton ever done anything the easy way?

'Gravesen had already been booked when Simonsen sprawled to block Malbranque's low drive, then a second over-exuberant challenge saw Barber flourish his 70th yellow card of the season and the siege began.

'Ferguson importantly headed one effort off his own goalline on the stroke of half-time, and Everton stoutly defended their goal for a further seven minutes after the restart.

'Then Steed Malbranque stabbed in Fulham's lifeline after Hayles had wheeled away from Hibbert and pulled back a cross, but the Blues refused to buckle.

'They did creak – and came perilously close when Saha's looping header slapped the face of the crossbar with five-and-a-half minutes remaining, but for once even fortune smiled on the Toffees.

'David Moyes will now have a full week to work with his charges before the next cup final, at Pride Park on Saturday. But they will go there buoyant.

'Before we get too carried away, though, winning Goodison starts for new Everton managers are not rare. Even the hapless Mike Walker walloped Swindon Town 6-2 on his Goodison bow.

'The last Blues' boss who didn't manage a winning start was Walter Smith. But thoughts of the last Everton manager were miles away on Saturday. This was all about new starts, fresh ideas and bold impetus.

'If that proves enough to keep Everton in the top flight to celebrate their 100th season in England's most elevated echelon, Bill Kenwright will have got it right.

'By five o'clock on Saturday, though, most of Goodison Park had already made their minds up.'

MATCH STATS

EVERTON: Simonsen, Hibbert, Weir, Stubbs, Pistone, Gemmill, Gravesen, Carsley, Unsworth (Blomqvist), Ferguson, Radzinski (Moore).

FULHAM: Van der Sar, Finnan, Brevett, Melville, Goma (Ouaddou), Malbranque, Collins, Legwinski (Goldbaek), Boa Morte (Hayles), Marlet, Saha.

GOALS: EVERTON Unsworth (1), Ferguson (12)
FULHAM Malbranque (52)
ATTENDANCE 34,639

People's Club Songbook

CHAPTER 4

The songs and chants
made famous by
the People's Club

18 78

NIL SATIS NISI OPTIMUM

Everton

'When the chips are down and a 12th man is needed, the Gwladys Street choir can usually be relied upon'

EVERTONIANS have always been different.

Just look at their choice of pre-match music.

While other clubs choose to run out to supposedly inspiring classical tracks, constantly changing pop anthems - or a dirge from Carousel, Everton chose the soundtrack to a 1960s police series.

Why Z-Cars? Well it's undeniably infectious, but it's not exactly a song to sing along to.

But Blues fans don't care.

The *Z-Cars* theme tune, an adaptation of Johnny Todd, is unique. It is distinctive.

And the programme from which it was taken is indelibly associated with Merseyside.

That programme was also a real kick up the backside for establishment television in the 1960s, providing a rebellious counter to cosy and safe police shows like *Dixon Of Dock Green*.

Evertonians have always related to that ideal.

They may not sing incessantly and unnecessarily, like the inhabitants of the ground we abandoned in 1892, like Portsmouth or the Sheffield Wednesday band.

But when the chips are down and a 12th man is needed, the Gwladys Street choir can usually be relied upon. Listen to Phil Neville, after a 10-man Everton team overcame the early sending off of goalkeeper Iain Turner to beat Blackburn Rovers in 2005-06:

"You wouldn't get an atmosphere in any other ground like you had here at Goodison on Saturday," he declared. "It was really special. Somebody said at half-time it was the kind of circumstance made for Everton Football Club. You could see at the end it is probably embroidered in the club's tradition now."

It's a tradition which stretches back to the days when Queen Victoria sat on the throne of England and footballers wore walrus moustaches.

Here we try to give you just a flavour of the wit and the passion of the Goodison crowd, in just a selection of the songs sung by the Royal Blue choir down the years.

The earliest reference ever found to any song sung by an Everton crowd came at the 1893 FA Cup final against Wolves. It may even point towards the origins of mass singing at football matches:

As I walk along the Bois Boulong
With an independent air
You can hear the girls declare
He must be a millionaire
You can hear them sigh and wish to die
You can see them wink the other eye
At the man who broke the bank at Monte Carlo

Community singing almost became compulsory at Cup finals, and towards the end of Everton's first successful final appearance in 1906, the Evertonians in the Crystal Palace crowd chanted (according to contemporary reports):

'Och Aye, Sandy Scored a Goal'

By the 1920s football chants had become more relative to individual clubs and players, and it was no surprise that Dixie Dean figured in many:

After the ball was centred
After the whistle blew
Dixie got excited
And down the wing he flew
Passed the ball to 'Geldard'
And 'Geldard' shot it in
Left the poor goalie
Lying on his chin

Of course the catchphrase "Give it to Dixie" had first been coined during the young legend's rise to prominence at Tranmere Rovers, but it was never more appropriate than on the day Dixie scored his 60th league goal against Arsenal in 1928. Everton were awarded a penalty with Dean on 58 goals.

The chant immediately sprang up all around the ground of:

Give it to Dixie
Give it to Dixie
Give it to Dixie

They did, and Dixie promptly responded by rattling in goal number 59 for the season and levelling George Camsell's record.

Talk about "The People's Club" and one song immediately springs to mind. If you know your history is all about being the first club in the city and it's one that Evertonians are happy to remind their neighbours of...

It's a grand old team to play for,
It's a grand old team to support,
And if yer know your history,
It's enough to make your heart go woooooooow

We don't care what the red side say,
what the heck do we care?
Cos we only know that there's gonna be a show,
And the Everton boys will be there...

Five years later, during Everton's first visit to Wembley Stadium, the Blues fans chanted:

E-V-E-R-T-O-N
That's the place that means heaven to me
E-V-E-R-T-O-N
And blue is the colour of the jersey
E-V-E-R-T-O-N

And we'll bring the Cup back home again next year
When you put it altogether it spells EVERTON
That's the place that means home sweet home to me

By the 1950s, songs were becoming increasingly more complex
and original, like the following terrace compilations:

Our half-back line
Is strong and firm
Our captain's a fine fellow
So raise your glass
And give a cheer
For Farrell, Jones and Lello

Now is the hour
For me to say goodbye
Soon I'll be sailing
Far across the sea
While I'm away

Oh please remember me
When I return
I'll find you waiting here

Come on Blues

Come on Blues

Come on Blues

Marching down the Goodison Road
All the windows opened wide
When you hear the copper shout 'hey, put that candle out'
We are the Goodison gang
We have no manners, we spend our tanners
We are respected, wherever we may go
Marching down the Goodison Road
All the windows opened wide
When you hear the copper shout 'hey, put that candle out'
We are the Goodison guys
All the fans fall for Eddie Wainwright
And their thousands shout encore
For there's magic in Eddie Wainwright
That makes you want to roar
He's fast and clever, he bangs that leather
He's the Toffees' pride and joy
He strives with might and main
We might be on that Wembley train

Hip hooray, Eddie boy!

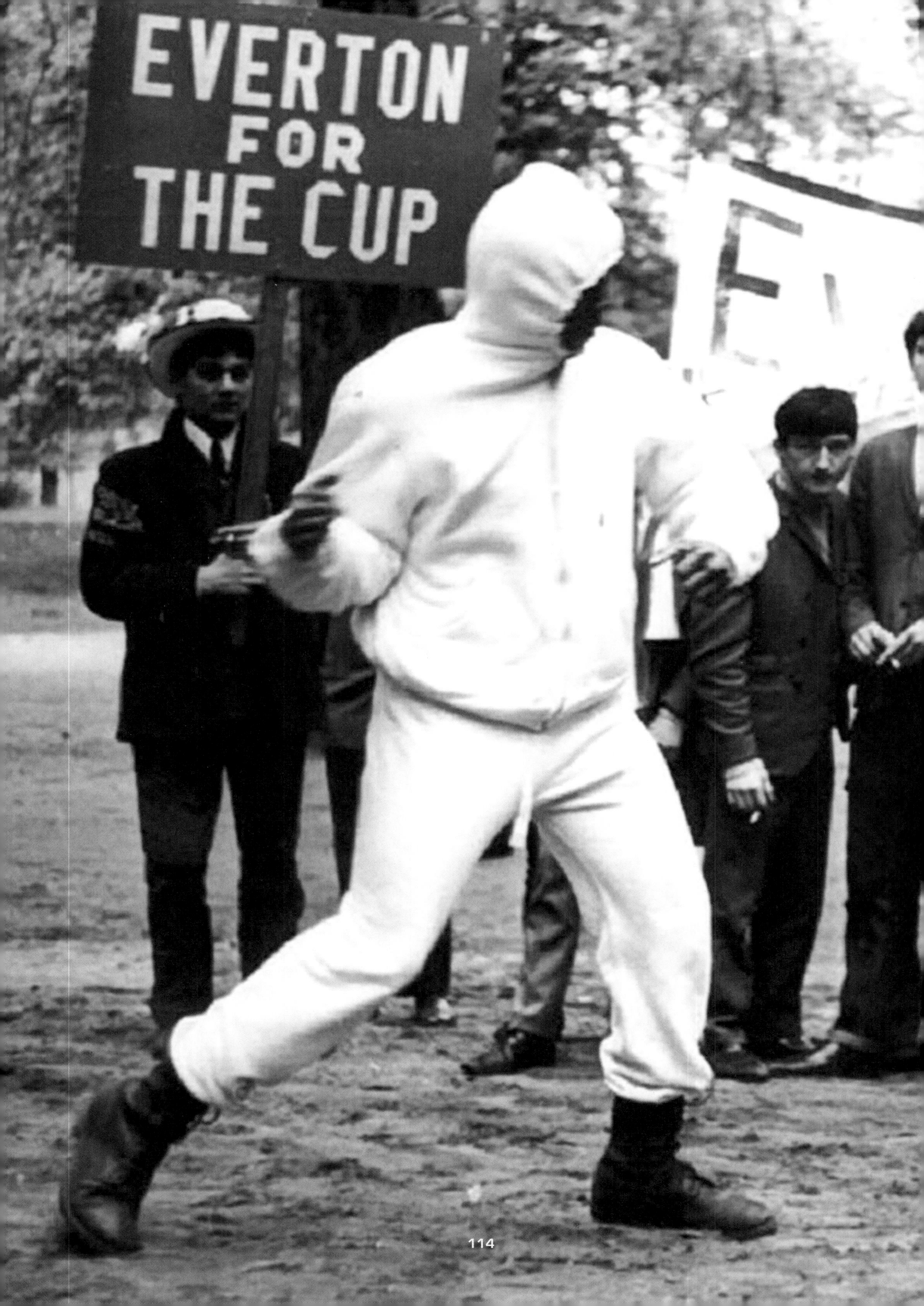
EVERTON
FOR
THE CUP

One of the simplest, but most effective Everton chants emerged in the 1960s, and was inspired by one of the greatest sportsmen of all-time. Muhammad Ali was pictured enjoying a mock sparring session with Blues fans in Hyde Park prior to his contest with Henry Cooper and Everton's Cup final showdown with Sheffield Wednesday. A year later, the link established, Ali fought Ernie Terrell, a fighter who refused to acknowledge Ali's name change from his old slave-name of Cassius Clay. Ali hurt Terrell badly. And each time he hit him he asked Terrell, "What's my name?" Cue a hugely popular chant from Blues fans:

What's our name? EVERTON! What's our name? EVERTON!

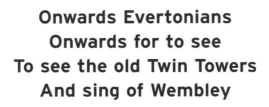

"We shall not be moved" was another song inspired by events across the Atlantic.
A song of defiance sung by the civil rights movement in the USA, it seemed to echo the rebellious and edgy mood
growing on the terraces of English football in the 1960s.

Onwards Evertonians
Onwards for to see
To see the old Twin Towers
And sing of Wembley

See the Royal Blue jerseys
As graceful as can be
Forging on to victory
And fighting constantly

Onwards Evertonians
Don't let your pride be moved
Remember our song for Wembley is 'We Shall Not Be Moved'

We shall not, we shall not be moved
We shall not, we shall not be moved
Just like the team that's gonna win the FA Cup
We shall not be moved

By the 1970s and beyond, almost anything seemed to go. Ballads were sung in one breath, followed by belligerent,
aggressive goading of opposition fans in the very next. Here's a cross-section.

You are my Everton
My only Everton
You make me happy
When skies are grey
You'll never know just
How much I love you
So please don't take
My Everton away

Na na,
na na
naaaa

The Blues are coming up the hill boys
The Blues are coming up the hill
They all laugh at us
They all mock at us
They all say our days are numbered
Born to be a Scouser
Victorious are we
So if you want to win the Cup
Then you better hurry up
'Cos we are Everton FC
Victorious and glorious
We'll take the Spion Kop
Between the four of us
And glory be to God

What's our
name? (Everton)
What's our
name? (Everton)...

Oh I heard Bertie Mee say to Bob Paisley
Have you heard of the North Bank Highbury
Bob says no, I'll tell you what though
I've heard of the Street End Aggro

As the glory days of the 1980s kicked into action,
this ditty was popular at Christmas time:

On the first day of Christmas
my true love gave to me
A Neville Southall in goal
On the second day of Christmas
my true love gave to me
Two Gary Stevens and a Neville Southall in goal
On the third day of Christmas
my true love gave to me
Three Psycho Pats, Two Gary Stevens, and a Neville Southall in goal
On the fourth day of Christmas
my true love gave to me
Four Kev the Rats, Three Psycho Pats,
Two Gary Stevens, and a Neville Southall in goal
On the Fifth Day of Christmas
my true love gave to me
Five Derek Mountfields ...
Four Kev the Rats, Three Psycho Pats, Two Gary Stevens,
and a Neville Southall in goal
On the Sixth Day of Christmas
my true love gave to me
Six Peter Reid, five Derek Mountfields ...
Four Kev the Rats, Three Psycho Pats, Two Gary Stevens,
and a Neville Southall in goal
On the Seventh Day of Christmas
my true love gave to me
Seven Tricky Trevs, Six Peter Reids, five Derek Mountfields ...
Four Kev the Rats, Three Psycho Pats, Two Gary Stevens, and a
Neville Southall in goal etc.

The Everton boys are the cock of the north
We hate Man United and City of course
We only drink whisky and bottles of brown
The Everton boys are in town

Oh when you're smiling, when you're smiling
The whole world smiles with you
And when you're laughing, when you're laughing
The sun comes shining through
But when you're crying, you'll bring on the rain
So stop your crying
Be happy again
'Cos when you're smiling
When you're smiling
The whole world smiles with you...
...without yer kecks on!

Show them the way to go home
They're tired and they don't know what to do
'Cos they're only half a football team
Compared to the boys in blue

Evertonians have always been quick to coin or alter songs to fit specific circumstances.
In 1966, with Goodison Park a stage for some of the most spectacular matches of the World Cup finals, local fans came up
with their own reaction to some of the world stars they had seen grace Goodison:

Bless 'em all,
Bless 'em all
The long and the short and the tall
Bless wee Alex and Royston too
Bless all the boys who are wearing the blue
Bless 'em all,
Bless 'em all
The crowds on the terraces call
Come on you Blues, you'll never lose
Bless 'em all, bless 'em all,
Bless 'em all

When I was young
A Park End boy I wanted to be
So I said ta-ra, to my Ma and Da
And left in my Everton jersey
I sailed with the Stanley sailors
Aboard the good ship Victory
And we sailed down Scotty Road
In a black Maria van
Oh Scotty Road I am, forsaken
And it's not that my poor heart is aching
Oh it's the whisky and the rum
We've all been taking from my Mum
And that charming little Toffee Girl
Down on the Scotty Road

Oh SCOTTY ROAD

Alan Ball never wore No. 9 on his back, or scored a goal which
saved the Blues from relegation, but he never needed to.
He was idolised at Everton from the second he signed for Everton in 1966,
through to his tragically premature death in 2007...and beyond.

**Who's the greatest of them all
Little curly Alan Ball
Who's the one we love the most
Alex Young the Holy Ghost**

**Five years after Harry
had been at Everton
He signed Alan Ball from Blackpool
Now Alan Ball plays for Everton
And now Alan is the greatest of them all
Ob-la-di, ob-la-da, Alan Ball oh
He's the greatest of them all
Ob-la-di, ob-la-da, Alan Ball oh
He's the greatest of them all**

**Now we're off to Wembley
to win the FA Cup
See the Twin Towers as before
Watch Alan Ball grace the Wembley turf
And win the FA Cup once more
Ob-la-di, ob-la-da, Alan Ball oh
He's the greatest of them all
Ob-la-di, ob-la-da, Alan Ball oh
He's the greatest of them all**

**Aye, aye, aye, aye,
Oh West is better than Yashin
And Ball is better than Eusebio
Liverpool's in for thrashin'**

After the famous FA Cup fifth-round success over Liverpool in 1967, decided by Alan Ball's solitary strike,
the Gwladys Street quickly penned one of its most ambitious lyrics:

**Bill Shankly to Ron Yeats come listen my boy
I've devised this great plan that you're sure to enjoy
Those Everton Toffees we'll knock out the Cup
And a great celebration we'll have on the Kop**

**We'll kick Jimmy Husband, Joe Royle as well
We'll kick those blue Toffees, we'll kick them to hell
And the only man standing will be Brian Labone
And he can't beat 11 red shirts on his own**

**But alas Mr Shankly, your plan it went wrong
And even your Kopites could not raise one song
For the man they forgot was the greatest of all
That red-headed dynamo named Alan Ball**

**In the 44th minute of a goalless report
Smith, Yeats and Lawrence on the wrong foot were caught
A square ball from Husband with great force was met
By the boots of young Alan to the back of the net**

**So listen you Kopites, for you must agree
Yours is the dirtiest team that you'll see
And to beat those blue Toffees, you first must report
To the blue and white Street End who give their support!**

Then there was the truly bizarre chant of the mid-1970s which was usually accompanied
by a frenetic, surge of fans bouncing down the middle of the Gwladys Street...not a place for the faint-hearted.

**I'm a bow-legged chicken and a knock-kneed hen,
I haven't had a fight since I don't know when
I walk with a wiggle, and a waddle and a squawk
Doing the Everton boot walk
Na, na, na, naa, naa, naa, naa, naa, naa**

Doing the Everton boot walk!

THE **SONGS** & **CHANTS**

During the 1977 League Cup campaign which took Everton to Wembley for the first time in nine years, Evertonians produced a simple but effective chorus:

Tell me Ma, me Ma
I don't want no tea, no tea
We're going to Wembley
Tell me Ma, me Ma!

But by the spring of that season, and Everton also in the semi-finals of the FA Cup, it quickly became apparent that the original lyrics had been overtaken by events and a new version was needed. The Gwladys Street lyricists were up to the challenge and the chant quickly became:

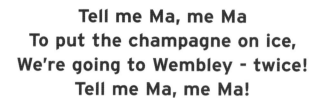

Tell me Ma, me Ma
To put the champagne on ice,
We're going to Wembley - twice!
Tell me Ma, me Ma!

In the 1980s, with Everton appearing at Wembley seemingly every couple of months, another version also appeared which included: "Tell me Ma, me Ma, to get in a crate of beer, it's Wembley three times this year, Tell me Ma, me Ma."
The FA Cup and visits to Wembley always seemed to bring out the best in the Evertonian imaginations.
Like this reflection on Liverpool's 2-1 defeat of Leeds United in the 1965 final, followed by Everton's dramatic 3-2 victory over Sheffield Wednesday the following year:

It was on a dirty Saturday in the dirty month of May
That they all went down to Wembley
To see the red side play
There was Callaghan and St John
And they played in dirty red
And half-an-hour before the end
The Queen went home to bed
It was on a sunny Saturday in the merry month of May
That we all went down to Wembley
To see the Toffees play
There was Alex Young and Gabriel
And they played in Royal Blue
And we gave the Wednesday a two-goal start
And we still beat them three-two
Now when Brian went up to receive the Cup
The sun was shining fine
It was the third time that we'd won the Cup
And we didn't need extra time

Evertonians had always worshipped their idols, and the man wearing the No. 9 jersey was usually the recipient of the loudest praise. Like:

Who's the player with precision
Alex Young the Golden Vision

Or:

Born in a barn in Ellesmere Port
The rules of football he was never taught
Got sent off when he was only three
For giving the ups to the referee
Davey, Davey Hickson
King of the transfer list

In 1978, with Bob Latchford closing on the first 30-league goal haul for six seasons and a £10,000 prize from a national newspaper, Blues fans adapted Lena Martell's No. 1 pop song of the time to fit his goal chase:

One goal at a time, Bob Latchford,
That's all we're asking of you.
If you hit the bar,
We'll all go aah,
One goal at a time

After Barry Horne's dramatic, swerving 25-yarder which helped spark the incredible fightback against Wimbledon in 1994, the following song swept Goodison Park:

Who needs Cantona when
we've got Barry Horne!

Alex Young, Alex Young,
We all love you Alex Young
He's a true blue and we all love you
What a player is Alex Young

Graeme Sharp,
Superstar
Scores from miles out
Past Grobbelaar

Follow, follow, follow
Everton's the team to follow
There's nobody better than
Mikel Arteta
He's the best little
Spaniard we know

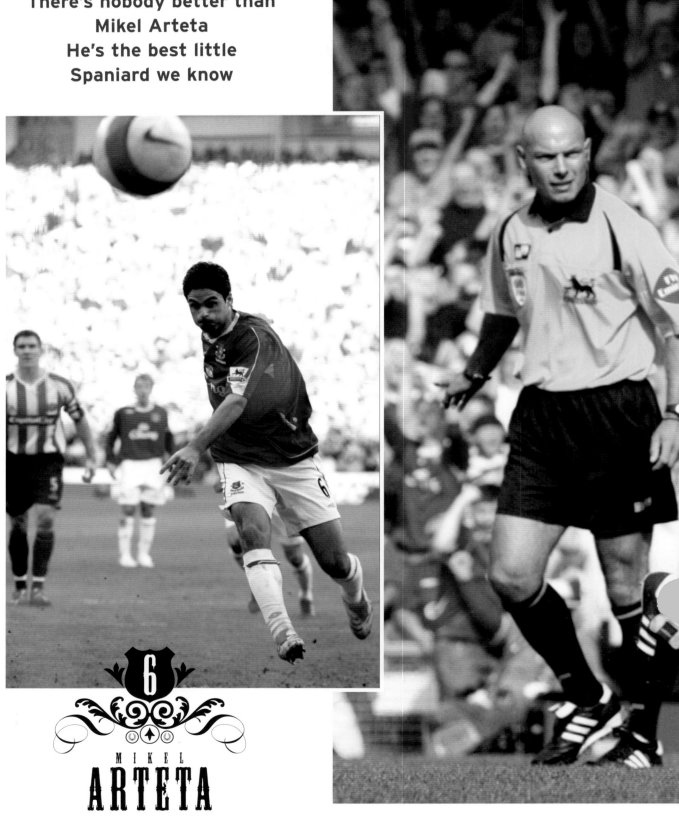

MIKEL
ARTETA

People's Club Managers

CHAPTER 5

Stories of the men
who have been in the
Goodison hotseat

'He had the ability to open doors that were closed to other people'

Theo Kelly 1939-1948

THEO Kelly holds the distinction of becoming Everton's first-ever manager in 1939, but he never enjoyed the full responsibilities attached to the role.

Everton had been one of the last clubs in English football to appoint a full-time manager, preferring a selection panel made up of senior coaches, boardroom executives and specially-appointed committees.

And while Kelly was promoted from secretary to manager in the wake of the 1938-39 title success, he was still effectively a figurehead with many of the important decisions still being made by committee.

It was a turbulent reign, with Kelly's prior track record already suggesting he was not an individual to whom man-management came easily.

Kelly had largely been responsible for Dixie Dean being sold to Notts County, stranded on 399 league matches and 349 goals.

"This chap Kelly had no time for the older lads, especially me," explained Dean.

"I just couldn't get on with him. He was secretary but I didn't care what he was. I knew what was happening.

"He wanted to get rid of me and also one or two other people who looked like being in with a chance of becoming manager one day."

Joe Mercer, a Sergeant-Major during the War, was another who might have fitted that bill and indeed went on to become a highly-respected manager of Aston Villa, Manchester City and England.

But he explained: "Theo Kelly was the manager and I had one or two ups and downs with him.

"The funny thing was he wanted me to play centre-half – me, a wing-half who used to go diving into the action, when the club had T. G. Jones, the best centre-half of all in my opinion.

"Things became so bad between Theo and me that one day I went to see the directors at the old Exchange Hotel, where they heard the board meetings, and said 'Transfer me, or I turn it in.'

"The directors said they wanted me to stay, but I was determined and Arsenal paid £9,000 for me."

But Harry Catterick put Kelly's contribution into perspective when he explained: "He was the best public relations man I have ever known and any shortcomings he might have had with the players were compensated by his ability to open doors that were closed to other people."

His first seven years as manager found him in charge of a team playing War-time regional football, and when the Football League resumed he also found himself swiftly having to do without star centre-forward Tommy Lawton, who insisted on moving south to Arsenal.

After two disappointing seasons – and a wretched start to the 1948-49 campaign, the Blues' board bowed to pressure from their fans and the media and appointed a new manager.

Old favourite Cliff Britton returned to the club he had graced as a player, while Kelly reverted to his old job of secretary.

Mr. THEO KELLY

Born Liverpool 1896. Educated Walton Lane Council School and Oakes' Institute. Joined the Everton club August 1929, to succeed the late Mr. D. Kirkwood. Appointed Assistant Secretary 1934, and subsequently as acting-secretary during the long illness of the late Mr. McIntosh.

Ten years Hon. Secretary Orwell Wednesday F.C. Served in the Navy during the war. Keen worker for football in all its branches, and a clever judge of players in the embyro stage.

Quite a number of Mr. Kelly's youthful "signings" have since made good in Evertons' League side.

The new secretary is an elder son of Mr. Louis T. Kelly, and brother-in-law to Mr. Tom Bromilow the Crystal Palace manager.

'His ideal Everton team would have been made up of 11 teetotal bachelors'

WHEN the Everton board relented and appointed a new full-time manager in September 1948, their choice was universally popular.

Cliff Britton had been a respected and admired wing-half at Everton throughout the 1930s, making 240 appearances for the club, claiming an FA Cup winners' medal in 1933 and winning nine England caps.

He added 12 more caps to his collection in War-time internationals, figuring in a polished half-back line alongside Joe Mercer and Stan Cullis, then as a rookie manager guided Burnley from Division Two to third place in the First Division, plus the FA Cup final at Wembley.

He had all the credentials to help guide a proud club back to its place amongst the elite of English football, but it was never a happy reign.

"Cliff Britton was hard but fair," recalled winger Tommy Eglington. "His ideal team would have been made up of 11 teetotal bachelors.

"We were bitter about the way things ended up for him at Goodison."

Well liked by fans and players alike, the closest he came to glory was when his team reached the semi-final of the FA Cup in 1950, then again in 1953.

Liverpool were the victors in 1950, going on to lose in

Cliff Britton   1948-1956

the final against Arsenal at Wembley, while three years later Everton found themselves 4-0 down to Bolton Wanderers, before astonishingly battling back to reduce the arrears to 4-3 and being left to bemoan an earlier missed penalty by Tommy Clinton.

However, that 1953 Cup run came as a Second Division club after Everton had crashed out of the top flight at the end of a grim 1950-51 campaign.

Everton needed a point from their final match to ensure safety. They crashed 6-0 at Sheffield Wednesday and spent three seasons in the wilderness before climbing back up as runners-up in 1953-54.

Once again, however, the all pervading presence of members of the board could be felt in the background.

Britton parted company with the club in 1956, following a dispute over Everton wanting to appoint an acting-manager while Britton was abroad with the team.

He left, saying: "I want all managers to have the freedom to do the job for which they were appointed, which is to manage their clubs."

Popular choice: Cliff Britton (right)

First-team coach:
Ian Buchan (left)

'Buchan stopped the coach two miles from the ground and made us walk'

A FORMER Scottish amateur international, Ian Buchan was appointed as first-team coach in August 1956, primarily to work with the players on fitness.

A revolutionary thinker, his ideas were a little ahead of his time.

One of his early psychological ploys was to order the players off the team coach two miles from Elland Road ahead of their opening match of the 1956-57 season at Leeds United, and to jog the rest of the way.

The idea was to intimidate the Leeds players into believing they were physically inferior to Everton.

One of those players was Tommy Eglington, and he later revealed how the thinking backfired.

"Ian Buchan was a fitness fanatic and he put us all on weight training," he said.

"I can remember going to play a match at Leeds when

Ian Buchan   1956-1958

John Charles was their centre-forward, and Buchan stopped the coach two miles from the ground and made us walk to keep us fit.

"We were passing our own supporters. Leeds riddled us with goals in the first half and at half-time one of our players cracked: 'It's a good job we're fitter than they are!'"

The final score was Leeds United 5, Everton 1 and Buchan's reign rarely threatened to improve.

After finishing 15th and then 16th, the Blues' board were forced to think again – and this time they appointed a man who would finally enjoy the full trappings of manager.

'He insisted (in the taxi) that he wanted to know what I had to say to him'

Johnny Carey   1958-1961

EVEN today, to suggest that a taxi should be hailed for an Everton manager is a suggestion that the clock is ticking on his employment prospects.

The saying goes back more than 40 years, to the time when likeable Irishman Johnny Carey was appointed manager of Everton Football Club.

A calm, assured footballer and a member of Matt Busby's first great Manchester United side, he brought those same qualities to the manager's chair at Ewood Park.

After five years as boss of Blackburn Rovers, he was head-hunted by Everton and, was both fortunate and unfortunate to arrive at the club at the same time as millionaire benefactor John Moores.

The good fortune came in the club's sudden ability to afford the very best players in the country.

After assessing what he had inherited, Carey fashioned the nucleus of an exciting team and was the man responsible for buying Alex Young, Roy Vernon, Jimmy

Gabriel and Alex Parker.

In 1960-61, after two lowly league campaigns, Everton finished fifth and there appeared to be genuine grounds for optimism.

However, new chairman John Moores, the man who had done so much to finance those transfer deals with an initial interest-free loan of £56,000, was impatient for genuine success.

He sacked Carey as the two sat in the back of a taxi following a Football League meeting in London.

"Somehow or other (word) had got around that we were dissatisfied with Johnny," recounted Moores. "After the meeting journalists were all around Johnny and all ears were cocked. I suggested to Johnny that we should go along to our hotel, The Grosvenor House, and we got a taxi. I wanted to discuss the matter with Johnny when we arrived at the hotel, but he insisted during the journey that he wanted to know what I had to say to him.

"It was then that I told him I wanted to discuss his position as manager, to see if it wouldn't be best for everyone if he left with a golden handshake.

"When we arrived at the hotel we talked for about an hour and finally decided it was best for Johnny to leave.

"I had nothing against Johnny, who was a nice man, an honourable man and a good practitioner, but we felt that we needed to make a change."

Thus, the phrase "Taxi for Carey" entered Mersey folklore.

'A strict disciplinarian, his signing-in book became legendary'

Harry Catterick   1961-1973

IN order to justify the sacking of a manager who had just guided his team to fifth in the First Division, Everton needed to find a manager from the very top drawer.

They found him in Harry Catterick.

He was not as outspoken or as charismatic as his managerial rivals Bill Shankly and Matt Busby, but he didn't need to be.

His teams were eloquent on his behalf.

He was handed a simple brief by John Moores: get Everton back to the very top by means of good, entertaining football. He succeeded on both counts.

A strict disciplinarian, his signing-in book at the club's Bellefield training ground became legendary. Joe Royle was a player who remembers the rigid routine clearly.

"Bellefield was run more like a strict public school than a soccer training ground," he recalled. "Every player, be he a junior or senior, was required to sign in by the appointed time: kids by 9am, seniors by 10am. If you were as little as one minute late you suffered the standard penalty, a fine of one day's wages. It was always rigorously imposed.

"Gordon Watson, a member of the backroom staff, would position himself in the doorway to the dressing rooms, book in hand, watching the entrance to Bellefield. If you drove through the gates bang on either of the deadlines, that was that – too late.

"That meant you would be signing in fractionally behind time. And, under Harry's law, the penalty for 30 seconds was the same as for 30 minutes. There was simply no excuse. One Monday morning Gordon West, John Hurst and Roger Kenyon, who all lived in Blackpool, came in late after being delayed by a bad accident on the motorway. They went immediately to Catterick's office to plead for leniency.

"Their problem was that there was no such thing as an extenuating circumstance to Catterick, who listened before asking: 'What time did you leave after the match

'With Catterick held in awe, rather than affection – one twitch of the Venetian blinds of his office was enough to put a spring in the step of even the most senior player – Everton finished fourth in his first season, then the following season were crowned as champions'

on Saturday?' They were puzzled by the question.

"Harry explained: 'Look, the game finished at 4.40pm and you've had from that time on Saturday until 10 o'clock this morning to get in for training. You are late. Fined one day's wages.'"

It was a regime which proved spectacularly successful.

With Catterick held in awe, rather than affection – one twitch of the Venetian blinds of his office was enough to put a spring in the step of even the most senior player – Everton finished fourth in his first season in charge, then the following season were crowned champions for the first time in almost a quarter-of-a-century. It was merely the precursor to a decade which produced some of the finest football Evertonians had ever seen.

Champions in 1963, Everton finished outside the top six just once that decade, the season they won the FA Cup in 1966. But it was the quality of the football Catterick's side produced which caught the eye as much as the results. During the years 1968 through to 1970 particularly, Everton sparkled, with the midfield triumvirate of Ball-Harvey-Kendall eliciting gasps of delight everywhere they played.

But as the 1970s dawned, the health of his side suffered and Catterick's own health was failing. He suffered a heart attack in 1972 and a year later it was decided to move him into an executive position.

He remained an Evertonian to his dying day and drew his last breath at Goodison Park watching an FA Cup tie against Ipswich Town in 1985.

'He smashed the British transfer record but glory days were far away'

ANOTHER former player, Billy Bingham, was the man entrusted with bringing stylish, title-winning football back to Goodison.

He almost carried out one half of his mission, leading the First Division title race throughout 1974-75, only to miss out when defeats by relegated sides Carlisle United and Luton Town proved costly.

But his teams were often labelled functional and the London press even called his title-chasing 1975 side 'robots.'

Perhaps as a counter to that criticism, Bingham brought in flair players like Duncan McKenzie and Andy King, but he was never around long enough to enjoy their talents.

McKenzie had only played five matches for his new

Billy Bingham   1973-1977

club when Bingham was sacked on January 10, 1977.

Bingham had enjoyed the full backing of his board. He smashed the British transfer record to land Bob Latchford in a £350,000 player-plus-cash deal in February 1974, then a few months later bought Martin Dobson in a straight £300,000 cash transfer.

But the glory days seemed as far away as ever and when he parted company with the club, his side was slumped in 13th place in the table.

With typical honesty and realism, he said: "If you're with a top club, you expect to be shot down."

'Everton weren't in a mess at that time, but they were certainly at a crossroads'

Gordon Lee   1977-1981

EVERTON turned to soccer trouble-shooter Gordon Lee in January 1977, a man with a reputation for sorting out clubs in a mess.

Everton weren't in a mess at that time, but they were certainly at a crossroads – and for two years Lee looked like turning the club around.

His fourth match in charge was a League Cup semi-final, second leg at Bolton Wanderers, and a soaring Bob Latchford header took Everton to Wembley.

They lost the final only in the last minute of extra time of the only English Cup final ever to require three matches to settle.

In the FA Cup he was just as unfortunate, a late 'winner' by Bryan Hamilton in an FA Cup semi-final against Liverpool being cruelly and incorrectly ruled out by Clive Thomas.

But the following season Lee started to construct a free-flowing and enterprising side which was a joy to watch.

Everton finished third in 1977-78 and were the division's highest scorers with 76 goals. Many came from the new partnership of Dave Thomas' direct wing-play and Bob Latchford's devastating finishing, and hopes were high that the Blues were on the brink of taking the next step to the title summit.

After an explosive start to the following season – 19 games unbeaten and a first victory over Liverpool for seven years – success looked a possibility, but when the pitches deteriorated, so too did Everton.

They finished a disappointing fourth, and while that was enough to ensure a second successive European campaign, it ended at the first time of asking with home and away defeats by Feyenoord.

Results and league position continued to slide and after a shocking 19th place in 1980, lifted only by a run to the semi-final of the FA Cup and defeat by Second Division West Ham, Lee's side finished 15th in 1980-81.

This time a run to the quarter-final of the FA Cup wasn't enough to save Lee, and he was sacked on May 6.

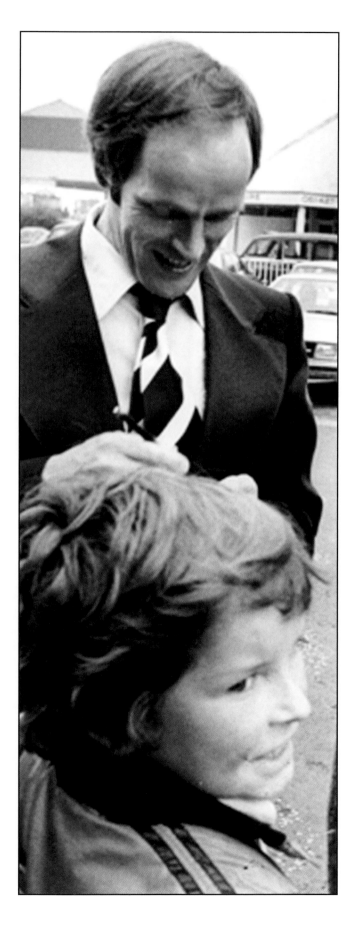

'He knew he wasn't first choice but that didn't faze Kendall'

SOME 13 managers have held the title manager of Everton Football Club.

None has been as successful as Howard Kendall.

His name is synonymous with the club and his famous statement: "If Manchester City was like a love affair, Everton Football Club is like a marriage to me," is utterly appropriate.

He was the man who gave Evertonians back their pride in the 1980s after a decade and a half of non-achievement.

In three years Everton claimed two league titles, an FA Cup and the European Cup Winners' Cup – and there should also have been a League and Cup double to celebrate, stolen from under Everton's noses in 1986 by rivals Liverpool.

The team that Howard built was the best in the land between 1984 and 1987.

Consequently the fans were stunned when, frustrated by the ban from European football, he decided to join

Howard Kendall 1981-1987 1991-1994 1997-1998

Athletic Bilbao in the summer of 1987, then looked on enviously when he returned to English football, but in the paler blue of Manchester City.

It was a sensation when he returned to Goodison Park in November 1990, but after initially arresting a slide down the table, he couldn't rekindle the same spark he had enjoyed just a few years previously. In December 1993 he resigned, disillusioned by the board's transfer policy, but his Everton career wasn't done yet.

In June 1997 chairman Peter Johnson turned to Howard Kendall for a third time. He knew he wasn't first choice, but that didn't faze Kendall as he characteristically set about trying to create an attractive passing team, promoting some of the club's talented youngsters and dipping frequently into the transfer market.

The fans remained patient with him, even if the chairman didn't, and by January it looked like Kendall was winning the battle when he was named Manager of the Month.

But it was a short-lived revival and as Everton plunged to the lower reaches of the table again, only a point from a home draw with Coventry City on a traumatic last day of the season prevented ignominious relegation.

Kendall and Everton parted company for the final time in the summer of 1998, although he remains the truest of Evertonians.

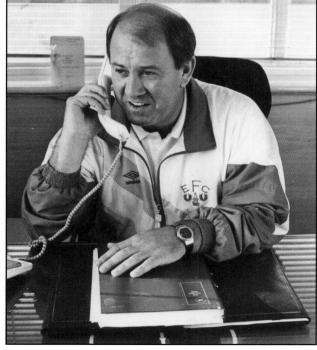

World team of the year: Picking up a prestigious award in 1985

'It's my time as a player that I will treasure more than anything'

A MAGNIFICENT coach who deserved much of the credit for Everton's spectacular success throughout the 1980s, he was the logical choice to succeed Howard Kendall when his mentor left for Spain in 1987.

In hindsight, his spell was more than creditable, but he was following the most successful, trophy-laden era in the club's history and was always on a hiding to nothing.

He won the FA Charity Shield in his first match as manager - defeating Coventry City at Wembley - reached the semi-final of the Littlewoods Cup and finished fourth in his first full season as manager, and that was seen as failure!

The next campaign saw a further slide to eighth and

Colin Harvey 1987-1990

defeat in the all-Mersey FA Cup final to Liverpool, then 1989-90 saw a sixth-place finish.

When the 1990-91 season started disappointingly, Harvey was saddened to find himself axed by the Blues' board, then delighted to accept his old role as No. 2 to Howard Kendall once again.

Always happier out of the limelight, he continued to offer yeoman service to the club as a youth coach and it was under his guidance that Everton won the FA Youth Cup in 1998, producing stars of the future like Francis Jeffers, Michael Ball and Richard Dunne, then reached the 2002 Youth Cup final, this time with a jewel like Wayne Rooney in their ranks.

He retired soon after and was rewarded with a richly deserved testimonial match in 2003 against Parma.

Despite his spell as a manager and coach, however, Harvey said: "It's my time as a player that I'll treasure more than anything else.

"To be an Everton supporter and go on to play almost 400 games for the first team means more to me than anything, and that's what's given me the biggest satisfaction."

'Only a dramatic last-day triumph over Wimbledon spared the blushes'

MIKE Walker's managerial reign was the shortest in Everton history – and while his belief in attractive, passing football never wavered, a parting of the ways was always inevitable.

He took over a club which had picked up just one point in seven matches as it plummeted managerless following Howard Kendall's resignation on December 4, 1993.

He was appointed in January 1994 and a 6-2 victory over Swindon Town briefly hinted at a revival.

But that was the season the Robins were relegated after conceding 100 goals, and Everton almost joined them through the top-flight trapdoor, only a dramatic last-day triumph over Wimbledon sparing the Toffees.

Mike Walker   1994

Walker spent heavily, recruiting gifted but fitful stars like Daniel Amokachi, Anders Limpar and Vinny Samways and failing in an ambitious bid for Brazilian striker Muller, then saw his side slump to the worst start to a season in Goodison history.

The fans never turned on him, but by November, with the club's place in the Premier League looking increasingly precarious, the boardroom finally lost patience and decided to part company.

It was not a match too soon.

'Everton soared to sixth, missing out on Europe in the dying minutes'

RARELY has a manager enjoyed such a stirring start to his managerial career as that enjoyed by returning hero Joe Royle in November 1994.

Everton were on death row, marooned at the bottom of the league with just one win from their opening 14 matches – and table-topping rivals Liverpool next-up at Goodison Park.

With hitherto ignored Andy Hinchcliffe, John Ebbrell and Joe Parkinson restored to the starting line-up, Everton scored an unlikely 2-0 triumph.

They followed up with another win at Chelsea and a 3-0 defeat of Leeds as a revival began in earnest – and they ended the season securing safety in the penultimate match of the season at Ipswich Town.

Even more remarkably, however, that match came 11 days before an FA Cup final appearance at Wembley against Manchester United. Paul Rideout's header brought the Cup back to Merseyside, the last major silverware celebrated by an Everton side – and a platform was established for a brighter future.

The following season, with Andrei Kanchelskis recruited

Joe Royle   1994-1997

from the beaten Cup finalists, Everton soared to sixth, missing out on a place in Europe in the dying minutes of the campaign. Then the following season Everton won at Derby County in December and were talked of as "dark horses for the title."

Sadly, the title push never materialised.

Injuries to Andy Hinchcliffe, Dave Watson and Joe Parkinson proved crucial, Everton slipped down the table and rumours of boardroom dissatisfaction with the manager began to emerge.

It was still a shock when Royle announced his resignation in March, following a meeting with chairman Peter Johnson. He left the club having enjoyed two years and two months of upwardly-mobile progress and an unbeaten record in derby matches against neighbours Liverpool, followed by three months of disappointment.

But he remains a hugely popular figure amongst Evertonians.

'With financial problems ... Smith struggled to build on progress'

Walter Smith 1998-2002

WALTER Smith took over a club in crisis – and provided much-needed stability during a turbulent time in the club's fortunes.

A shrewd talent-spotter and a canny wheeler-dealer in the transfer market, he brought international-class stars like Olivier Dacourt, John Collins and future World Cup winner Marco Materazzi to the club within weeks of arriving as Everton manager.

But after a solid start to his managerial career, a second half of the season slump saw a relegation battle loom until on-loan Kevin Campbell came riding into town on his knight's charger.

The following season was much improved, a top-half finish only snatched away on the final weekend of the season, but with financial problems forcing a rapid re-think of the club's transfer policy, Smith struggled to build on the progress of 1999-2000.

He still enjoyed stirring FA Cup runs, being beaten in the quarter-finals on three separate occasions, but it was the final reverse, a demoralising 3-0 defeat at Middlesbrough, which proved his death knell.

Walter Smith and Everton went their separate ways, but he went on to provide invaluable assistance to Sir Alex Ferguson at Manchester United, before reviving the fortunes of the Scotland national team and then later returning to what had always been his first love, Glasgow Rangers.

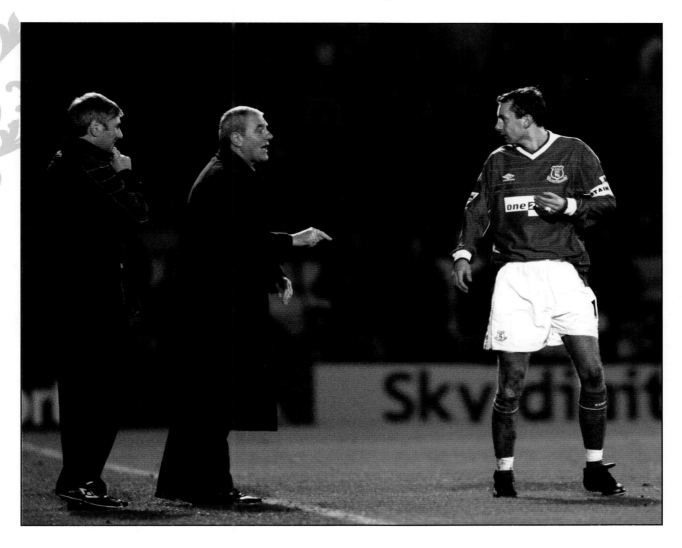

'I consider this move as getting as close to the top as you possibly can'

David Moyes 2002-

HE is the man who first coined the phrase "The People's Club." He is the manager who has twice been voted LMA Manager of the Year, he is the boss who has twice taken Everton back into European football and he is the coach who broke the big-four's stranglehold in the Premiership for the first time in years.

David Moyes has captured the imagination of Evertonians like few other managers. After bringing Preston North End to within a game of returning to the highest level of English league football for the first time in 40 years, he moved to Everton in March 2002.

The best: Getting a Manager of the Year award

His first match in charge was memorable, David Unsworth opening the scoring after 32 seconds, Thomas Gravesen being sent off, then the 10 men going on to win 2-1 against Fulham - and he quickly established a great rapport with the Goodison Park fans.

As well as his oft-repeated People's Club comment, at the press conference to announce his arrival, he added: "It's a great honour, something which I could only dream about. You start out in your career as a player and you try to get to the top, I consider a move to Everton as getting as close to the top as you possibly can."

The 2007-08 season saw Moyes celebrate his sixth anniversary at the club - making him Everton's third longest-serving manager in the modern era.

People's Club Cult Idols

CHAPTER 6

The players who
forged a special bond
with Evertonians

18 78

Everton

First man of the people

WILLIAM Ralph "Dixie" Dean was a true man of the people. So it was perhaps appropriate that he should become the first People's Club idol.

Of course, Evertonians had their heroes before Dean began sprinkling his stardust around Goodison Park – Victorian superstars like Nick Ross and Jack Sharp, Edwardian goalscorers like Alex "Sandy" Young and Jimmy Settle and free-scoring forwards like Bobby Parker, who fired the Blues to the 1915 Championship.

But Dean was different. He was a man of the people. He mixed with the fans, drank with them and shared their same experiences.

Bill Dean the actor, the man who played Harry Cross in *Brookside*, was actually born Patrick Connolly. But he decided to adopt his hero's name on stage in tribute to the man he idolised. And he explained the bond Dixie Dean had with the Everton fans.

"I chose my showbiz name Bill Dean because I was inspired by Dixie, the greatest Everton player of all time, the greatest centre-forward I've ever seen," he declared.

"Dixie didn't know how famous he was. The very fact he queued for the tram car in Water Street and then strolled into Goodison as if he was going for a kickabout

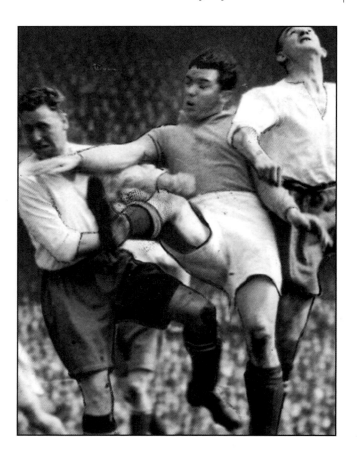

in the park underlines that. The day he scored his 60th he did exactly that."

The thespian Dean wasn't alone in his hero worship. Dean was idolised at home and abroad until the day he died.

A sign of a player's popularity during the 1920s and 1930s could be gauged by the number of cigarette cards printed bearing his image. Packets of cigarettes would carry a card, one of a set, and young boys would collect them and swap them in much the same way stickers are collected today.

Between 1925 and 1937 there were 28 cards published bearing Dixie Dean's name – more than any other British footballer. His closest rival at Everton was dual football and cricket international Harry Makepeace, with a mere 15. Dean's image appeared on cards issued in Australia and South Africa and his name was known the world over.

The great American baseball star, Babe Ruth, visited England and met Dean when he was playing at White Hart Lane in London.

Coincidentally, Ruth had hit a record 60 home runs for the New York Yankees in the same year that Dean scored his record-breaking 60 league goals.

Dean later recalled: "There was a lot of talk at the time about baseball becoming big over here and I think that's why Babe Ruth had come to England.

"He came to the match and was brought into our dressing room. As he walked in, he said in a loud voice: 'I just gotta meet this Dixie Dean guy!'

"We were introduced and I shook hands with him. He said to me: 'Your name's well known in the States even though we don't play your sport much.' I turned round and said: 'Well we know all about you in England, even though football and cricket are our big sports.'

"He asked me what cut I got of the game from that day's match. 'I don't get anything apart from eight pounds a week and another few bob if we win. That's what all the players are paid.' I don't think he could believe that and he said: 'See that crowd out there...it's as many as we get for a World Series game. I'd demand two thirds of the gate if I was out there.' I just said: 'You must be joking mate.'"

That was Dean to a tee. A man of the people. Ruth earned around £40,000 a season in 1930 and 1931, Dean less than £500. And he would spend some of that money in the pubs around Goodison Park on a Saturday night after he had usually fired the Blues to victory.

He joined Everton in 1925. It was almost 13 years later when he – reluctantly – left Goodison for Notts County. Not that other clubs hadn't tried to prise him away from Goodison in the meantime.

In 1932, some 70 years before Posh and Becks decamped to Real Madrid, reports from Spain suggested Real wanted the Everton hero.

A *Reuters* news report dated December 31, 1932, read: 'Football circles in Madrid are openly talking about the

possibility of Dixie Dean being approached on behalf of the Madrid Football Club to come to Spain as Madrid's centre-forward.

'No confirmation is available officially, but it is said that the secretary of the Madrid club wants to meet Dean in Paris to discuss the matter. Spanish footballers of the highest class are paid very high wages. Zamorra, the Spanish goalkeeper who was beaten seven times at Highbury when Spain played England on December 9, is in receipt of £25 per week. Dean would unquestionably be offered a similar wage. The Football League's maximum for English professionals is £8 per week, plus bonuses of £2 for a win and £1 for a draw.'

Dean's reaction to the news is unrecorded, but there was a direct quote from his wife Ethel. "This is the first I have heard of the offer for Billy to go to Spain," she said. "He is still sore from the bumping he received at Highbury and I am sure there is no truth in the story."

And that was that.

The Deans preferred to stay with their own people. Dean never left Merseyside his whole life. He frequently received letters and postcards from home and abroad, and after being asked to present the Footballer of the Year award to Kevin Keegan, the Press gave Dean a silver salver on which was inscribed: 'To Dixie Dean, 60 goals in a season, more than most teams score today.'

Dean stoops to head home in an FA Cup tie against Southport in 1931

'This is the first I have heard of the offer for Billy to go to Spain. He is still sore from the bumping he received at Highbury and I am sure there is no truth in it'

'Evertonians worshipped him. Those fans even tried to help him as he suffered from unnaturally sensitive feet which blistered. "I used to get all kinds of letters come to me suggesting things to do," he explained. "One, I remember, said I should pee on my feet"'

The Golden Vision

Golden vision: Young in action, and a fan makes his feelings known before a FA Cup tie against Sunderland in 1966

The Goodison Visionary

HARRY Catterick was the respected authoritarian figurehead of Everton Football Club throughout the 1960s.

But it says everything about the Messianic appeal of Alex Young that when he was left out for a league match at Blackpool in January 1966 to give 16-year-old Joe Royle his debut, angry supporters argued and jostled the Everton boss in the Bloomfield Road car park.

At least that was the story.

Young himself believed that Catterick had embellished the tale to avoid awkward questions about his decision to leave out the fans' favourite, and that he had simply slipped on ice during a harmless scuffle.

"Whoever said that has got it 100 per cent right," he declared. "I wasn't there, but I've spoken to a few of the players who were. One of them was Brian Labone, who quite liked Harry Catterick. He said nobody touched him; he slipped and fell on the ground and then got himself up.

"Catterick said hooligans assaulted him and he said that next week he would bring in what he called the hooligans' team, which meant Gordon West, Jimmy Gabriel and myself were back in the side.

"We went about 18 games undefeated after that and we won the Cup that year. The story from all the players that were there said that nobody assaulted Harry Catterick. Maybe somebody jostled him, but it wasn't any real assault."

The fans, however, were undoubtedly angry.

An iconic picture from the era shows a supporter being frogmarched off the Goodison Park pitch proudly parading a banner which reads:

'Sack Cattrick (sic) Keep Young.'

And this of a man who had brought the league title back to Goodison for the first time in 25 years!

But Young was a special footballer. He joined Everton in November 1960 from Hearts in a £55,000 deal that also brought his team-mate, full-back George Thomson, to Goodison Park and he soon won over the Blues' fans with his class. It was a reciprocal love affair.

"Goodison Park, to me, just seems to be a magical place, like when you go into certain houses where the great ghosts have been," said Young. "There was something there that made the back of my neck tingle when I ran onto the pitch for Everton, even when the place was empty.

"It's still the same whenever I visit. That tingle is still there - you can feel the vibes from the fans. I loved playing at home and that's why the majority of the games when I really turned it on were at Goodison Park. I could feel the goodwill coming from the fans.

"They've been so kind to remember me. They accepted me right from the very start and I'll never forget that. I always love going down to Goodison. I feel as if I'm going back home again."

In the Championship-winning season of 1962-63, Young scored in all three opening games, all wins, and ended the season with 22 goals to his name.

Arguably the greatest Scottish player ever to sign for Everton, he was a major influence in the team which over-turned Sheffield Wednesday in the FA Cup final of 1966. But it wasn't his match-winning abilities which inspired Evertonians, it was something slightly ethereal. It was his flair, his grace - and the distinctive shock of blond hair which earned him the nickname "The Golden Vision."

One of the classiest post-War Everton players, Evertonians worshipped him. Those fans even tried to help him as he suffered from unnaturally sensitive feet which blistered. "I used to get all kinds of letters come to me suggesting things to do," he explained. "One, I remember, said I should pee on my feet. Others said I should try methylated spirits and salt water. I tried everything - even the ancient cures. I used to get hundreds of letters wishing me well and there was none of them I didn't try because at that time I would have done anything!"

Evertonians would have done anything for Young.

He embodied the club he had joined, and personified The School of Science in many Evertonians' eyes.

Man who walked on water

BIG Bob Latchford was powerfully built, stood six feet tall and weighed 14 stone. But Evertonians believed he could walk on water.

For seven years the Gwladys Street battle anthem "Bobby Latchford Walks on Water" rang around Goodison Park, as Blues' fans discovered a centre-forward in the club's greatest traditions.

He arrived at Everton in February 1974 for a British record transfer fee, but the staggering figure of £350,000 – it was three-and-a-half years before it was broken – never weighed heavy on his shoulders.

He scored his first goal past Peter Shilton – with his left foot – in his third game, scored two more the following week against old club Birmingham City, then another at Burnley – and the supporters were smitten.

In his first full season he fired 17 league goals in 36 appearances, a campaign which promised to deliver the League Championship for long periods, but ultimately fell away when it mattered most.

The following season Latchford equalled a post-War scoring record by finding the net in seven successive league games, then top-scored once again with 25 goals in 1976-77.

A born opportunist, brilliant in the air with the near-post diving header a particular strength, he had a goalscorer's instinct which made him impossible to mark.

But it was when Gordon Lee enlisted the services of a specialist winger in the summer of 1977, the superbly direct Dave Thomas, that Latchford flourished.

A national newspaper, *The Daily Express*, was mourning the death of the out-and-out goalscorer and had offered a £10,000 cash prize for the first player to break the 30-league goal barrier, a mark which hadn't been breached for six seasons.

The challenge was right up Latchford's street.

Super Bob: The smiles on the fans' faces say it all

He took four games to open his account, broke his duck for the season at Leicester City, added typically swashbuckling headers against Manchester City and West Bromwich Albion – then went goal crazy at Loftus Road.

A stunning four-goal haul against Queens Park Rangers helped earn an England call-up, a thrilling hat-trick in a 6-0 demolition of Coventry City sealed it, then a brace against Middlesbrough ensured Latchford went into the New Year with 19 goals to his name.

As he closed on the total, he began to take penalties to augment his tally (Francis Lee had improved his total with 13 successful penalty-kicks in becoming the last player to score 30 league goals seven years previously).

Latchford needed two goals in the final match of the season against Chelsea to reach the total – and he got there with minutes to spare – sparking wild celebrations.

That was easily Latchford's most prolific season, and was the closest he came to title glory at Everton.

The Blues finished third – then fourth 12 months later, while dramatic goals in the League Cup final replay and second replay of 1977, and FA Cup semi-final replay of 1980 were both instances of what might have been.

Ultimately, his marksmanship procured no silverware during his spell at Everton, but he could point at one memorable achievement.

At a time when Liverpool dominated football domestically and abroad, Latchford enabled Evertonians to hold their heads with pride.

'At a time when Liverpool dominated football domestically and abroad, Latchford enabled Evertonians to hold their heads with pride'

'A born entertainer with a Pandora's Box of tricks, feints and dummies at his disposal, someone mentioned to McKenzie before his home debut against Birmingham City in December 1976: 'Do a few tricks and the fans will love you'

The born entertainer

HE flitted across the Goodison firmament fleetingly. But Evertonians all agreed that for the 61 games and 21 months he spent at Goodison Park, "Duncan McKenzie was Magic!"

A born entertainer with a Pandora's Box of tricks, feints and dummies at his disposal, someone mentioned to McKenzie before his home debut against Birmingham City in December 1976: "Do a few tricks and the fans will love you."

He did – and they did.

The fact that he scored twice, too, also helped.

But the McKenzie legend was firmly entrenched in Evertonian affections in an FA Cup tie against Stoke City three weeks later.

Supermac, as he was predictably christened, scored the match-clinching second goal in a 2-0 win – but it was a dribble from the corner of the Goodison Road side of the pitch, decorated with at least three dummied backheels, which the toiling Stoke markers fell for every time and which had the crowd in appreciative uproar.

The long, sinuous and mazy dribble was finally curtailed when he was fouled – on the Bullens Road side of the ground.

But the supporters adored it.

Perhaps adding to the McKenzie legend was the

Supermac: Duncan McKenzie's footballing philosophy clashed with that of Gordon Lee's

response on national television the next day.

The abrasive "Anfield Iron" himself, Tommy Smith – the very antithesis of McKenzie's football philosophy – had been invited to offer post-match analysis and select a Man of the Match.

"Well, no problems in choosing a man of the match then Tommy," smiled Elton Welsby.

"No," growled Smithy. "It's Andy King." He then went on to declare that McKenzie's talents would be better employed in a circus than on a football pitch.

McKenzie got his own back in an FA Cup semi-final at Maine Road, when he nutmegged Smith in a match notorious for Clive Thomas's incorrect decision to disallow Bryan Hamilton's late winner.

McKenzie also scored in that game, but his football philosophy never sat easily with that of the more stoic Gordon Lee, who had replaced Billy Bingham just a month after McKenzie's signing.

Despite forming a lively strike partnership with Bob Latchford, he was sold in September 1978 to Chelsea and replaced by big-money flop Mickey Walsh.

But the Everton fans didn't forget their hero.

He returned to Goodison with his new employers just six weeks later – opened the scoring for Chelsea, and was greeted with as loud a roar as if he'd still been wearing Royal Blue.

The Goodison gladiator

THERE'S a line in the science fiction film *Bladerunner* which sums up Andy Gray's Everton career perfectly.

Speaking to the renegade replicant Roy, engineering genius Tyrrel declares: "The light that burns twice as bright burns half as long. And you have burned so very, very brightly."

Andy Gray breezed into Goodison in November 1983. Barely 19 months later his Everton career was over. But Gray crammed more into that season-and-a-half than many players manage in an entire career – and as a result he was adored by Evertonians.

His spell at Everton might have come from the pages of a fictional novel.

When he arrived at Everton, the Blues were five places off the foot of the First Division, goals were in

desperately short supply and Howard Kendall's swoop for a supposedly burned-out striker with dodgy knees was seen as the act of a desperate man.

On his debut Gray chested a ball into Adrian Heath's path to set up a winning goal against Nottingham Forest, but it was the reaction which set Gray apart.

When somebody scored for Everton – anybody – Gray's face lit up and he was the cheerleader who ensured morale was sent soaring.

Just check out video recordings of the era – Gray is usually the first to celebrate with any goalscorer, eagerly beckoning his team-mates across to share in the joy.

At his peak Gray had been a top-class striker who once cost a British record-shattering transfer fee.

It was believed his best days had been and gone by the time Kendall swooped, but the Scottish gladiator enjoyed a glorious Indian Summer at Everton, his boldness and hunger for the ball enlivening team-mates on the pitch,

and his effervescent energy and charisma off it imbuing his team-mates with a confidence which had been hitherto hidden.

The effect and the influence he had on strike partner Graeme Sharp helped turn his international team-mate from promising youngster into top-class targetman.

His aerial ability and his braveness were matchless – and while Cup-tied for the Milk Cup campaign, he spearheaded an assault on Wembley in the FA Cup.

A diving header in the pouring rain at Notts County, where Gray slid in on his face to finish parallel with the floor as he diverted the ball into the County net, was legendary.

Two months later he connected with another flying header – via goalkeeper Steve Sherwood's fists – this time at Wembley, and a 14-year wait for silverware was finally over.

That trophy, however, was merely the catalyst for things to come.

Gray was an intermittent performer at the outset of the halcyon 1984-85 season but when Adrian Heath sustained a season-ending injury, he stepped in for the most thrilling spell of his entire career.

His performances were inspirational.

Flying headers against Sunderland defied belief, a hat-trick in a European Cup Winners' Cup quarter-final against Fortuna Sittard was classical – right foot, brave header, left-foot volley; a sizzling volley at White Hart Lane gave Everton a vital edge in the title race, then at Leicester City he buried a close-range header and was so desperate to race away and celebrate with his team-mates he ran straight into a goalpost! Undaunted, he bounced straight back up, blasted home a second, winning goal and his face beaming with joy became an iconic image for the BBC's *Match of the Day* programme.

That was just the start.

He scored in the European Cup Winners' Cup semi-final against Bayern Munich, added another in the final against Rapid Vienna – and earned himself a title winner's medal.

Bizarrely, with his popularity at its peak – Howard Kendall controversially replaced him with Gary Lineker.

There is little doubt Gray's best had been and gone, but Evertonians were still devastated by his departure and eternally grateful.

Hundreds upon hundreds wrote letters of support and thanks, so many that Gray had to respond via the pages of the *Liverpool Echo*.

Eighteen months later nearly 20,000 fans made the trip to Villa Park to cheer Everton onto the brink of a second league title in three years.

Kevin Sheedy's match-winner prompted the loudest roar of the day, but only just.

The travelling supporters were united in their appreciation of a man wearing claret and blue that afternoon...one Andrew Mullen Gray.

Warm welcome: Gray becomes acquainted with Rapid Vienna goalkeeper Michael Konsel, 1985

'When he arrived at Everton, the Blues were five places off the foot of the First Division ... Howard Kendall's swoop for a supposedly burned out striker with dodgy knees was seen as the act of a desperate man'

'He was sent off seven times in his Goodison career – but the first two were laughable and the third was for calling David Elleray a baldy b*****d. It was only when his body began to fail him and he became frustrated that flailing elbows and in one instance, a recklessly stupid punch, meant his suspensions began to be justified'

The Tartan talisman

THE world outside of Goodison Park could never understand Evertonian obsession with Duncan Ferguson. While critics cried "waster", Evertonians roared "world beater."

Doubters said he was an enigma, but Blues called him an inspiration. And when pundits said he was a "head case" Toffees made him their "head man."

There is no doubt that amongst the vast majority of Blues fans Ferguson was a Tartan talisman who could do no wrong, a footballing braveheart who regularly turned it on against Liverpool and Manchester United – and a player who loved the club so much he had a crest tatooed on his shoulder.

His refusal to speak to the Press added to his mystique, creating an air of mystery around the undoubted menace he carried onto a football field.

Standing six feet four and athletically built, when Ferguson was wound up and in the mood he was simply unstoppable in the air. But he was also a highly skilful technician capable of scoring goals from all angles, inside and outside the penalty area.

Ferguson broke his vow of silence when he joined Newcastle United in November 1998 – and his words underlined the bond he had with Evertonians.

"The support I received from the people of Liverpool when I was in jail was special," he told *The Evertonian* magazine. "Everton fans will be in part of my blood because of the way they stood by me. Their loyalty to me was one of the main reasons why I love Everton so much. I will always have fond memories of the club. Getting to captain the club and wearing the No. 9 shirt after so many other great names meant a lot to me. Maybe you don't realise how much at the time, but I did genuinely love the fans and the club.

"Hopefully they will see me as someone who put his heart into the club and did his best for them."

He also spoke when he returned to the club two years later – before resuming his Tartan trappist's mantle, this time for good.

His silence ensured he enjoyed an almost mystical aura in the game. But it also generated problems for him. That silence meant that even people inside the game never knew him properly – and he often fell victim to his reputation.

He was sent off seven times in his Goodison career – but the first two were laughable and the third was for calling David Elleray a baldy b*****d. It was only when his body began to fail him and he became increasingly frustrated with his physical condition that flailing elbows and in one instance, a recklessly stupid punch, meant his suspensions began to be justified.

That enigmatic aura, however, also created a sense of menace about him which unsettled opponents.

Before a half-fit Ferguson came on as a half-time substitute at Anfield in November 1996, it is recorded that the Liverpool management spent the entire half-time interval discussing how they could stop him.

They didn't – and Everton snatched a late draw.

When he came on as a late substitute at Old Trafford near the tail-end of his career, his first action was to run over to Rio Ferdinand and stand, quite deliberately, next to him. The memory of the pummeling Ferdinand took at his head and boots just eight months earlier still uppermost in his mind – Ferdinand quickly made himself scarce.

A glance at the bare statistics which accompany Duncan Ferguson's career do not tell his full story. Just 71 goals in 189 starts, plus a further 71 substitute appearances, are not the stats of a goalscoring legend.

But statistics cannot conjure up the sensation of seeing him dab on the Braveheart warpaint and go to war. In full cry, he was an inspiring sight.

And while those days were far less frequent in his second spell at the club, he turned back the clock in his penultimate season and gave a younger generation of Evertonians a glimpse at what their dads had been going on about.

His performance against Manchester United on April 20, 2005 was inspirational – and the goal he headed into the Gwladys Street net a reminder of what he used to do more regularly when he first arrived at the club. That was originally on-loan, under Mike Walker's stewardship.

But when his sacking led to the return of a former centre-forward to the club, Joe Royle, a bond between Ferguson and the fans was quickly forged.

He scored his first goal for the club against Liverpool, down at the Gwladys Street End – just 48 hours after being breathalysed for drink-driving.

Another towering header against Manchester United, again in the Gwladys Street goal, and accompanied by a shirt-twirling celebration cemented the love affair. And a series of monumental performances against United and Liverpool ensured he became a crowd hero.

"When I arrived at Everton Duncan, I felt, was coasting along," explained Royle. "He'd been on loan without really doing too much, looking tidy, but hadn't threatened goal.

"He scored his first goal in the derby game, and then went on to become a massive figure for us in first, escaping relegation, and then winning the FA Cup.

"He'd had injury problems along the way, but whenever Duncan was on the pitch, we were a danger to the oppposition. The night I told Peter Johnson, the then chairman, that we had to make his loan signing permanent was the night after the Liverpool game where Neil Ruddock had famously kicked Duncan, and he'd upset Dunc that day, and Duncan had come alive – and when he was in that kind of mood he was unplayable.

"He had all the stuff needed to become one of the great centre-forwards, and but for injuries and maybe other things, I don't think it ever quite worked for him.

"He was never a problem for me. Maybe in some of the 'smaller' games he needed a bit of motivation, a bit of 'jigging along' but if you had faith in Duncan, then he would always repay it."

Evertonians certainly had faith. And they remain convinced their faith was richly repaid.

Farewell to a hero: Saying his Goodison goodbyes and (above) a typical Dunc goal and celebration against Liverpool in 1997

People's Club Captains

CHAPTER 7

Men who have worn
the armband with
pride and distinction

18 78

Everton

NIL SATIS NISI OPTIMUM

MORE than 40 players have enjoyed the privilege of being named Everton club captain since League football began in 1888.

Many more have worn the armband in the absence of the designated club skippers through injury or suspension.

In this chapter we focus on all of Everton's club captains, plus some of the deputies who stepped in, the men who led the People's Club out into battle and the players who enjoyed the respect of their team-mates and their peers.

Nick Ross   1888-1889

NICK Ross was the first man to lead Everton into league battle, on September 8, 1888.

He is also recognised as one of the finest defenders ever to pull on an Everton jersey.

He bore the profile of a man who might have cleaned up Tombstone or Dodge City, was hard, cunning, clever and fast – and contemporary reports bore testament to his sparkling reputation.

"His teeth were discoloured, almost green near the gums", reported James Catton of the *Athletic News,* "and he hissed through them as he played.

"He was the demon back, the most brilliant back of his day, if not of all time.

"The best I ever saw."

Ross made just 19 league appearances for the Toffees, in the days the club played at Anfield, but is still recognized as one of the finest defenders that ground has ever witnessed.

Richard Boyle, one of the club's famous early Scottish exports

'He bore the profile of a man who might have cleaned up Tombstone or Dodge City, was hard, cunning, clever and fast – and contemporary reports bore testament to his sparkling reputation'

Andrew Hannah   1889-1891

PRIOR to moving to Merseyside, Andrew Hannah made a name for himself in his native Scotland as an all-round athlete. In particular he excelled in the running and the hop, step and jump events at the Highland Games. Signed by Everton in 1889, he was immediately appointed club captain and struck up a fearsome partnership with Dan Doyle.

He was Everton's first league championship-winning captain, also won the Scottish Cup with Renton, and holds the distinction of becoming the first captain of Liverpool.

Perhaps he still remembered his spell with the Toffees when, in the first-ever meeting between the sides, he handled the ball to allow Everton to take the lead from a free-kick!

Johnny Holt   1889-1892

EVERTON'S first England international, Holt was signed from arch-rivals Bootle in time for the start of the inaugural league campaign and was widely respected...and feared.

Nicknamed the "little Everton devil," he stood just five feet four inches and weighed 10 stone two pounds, but he was a fiercely committed competitor. 'He was an artist in the perpetration of clever minor fouls,' recorded Everton's original Jubilee historian Thomas Keates. 'When they were appealed for his shocked look of injured innocence was side-splitting.' He spent 10 years at Everton, making 252 appearances, before moving on to Reading.

Bob Howarth   1893-1894

AN immaculate right-back, capped five times by England during an age when England international matches were few and far between, Howarth was a cool, calm and collected customer with a timely tackle.

He had been a double winner with Preston in 1888-89, before joining the Blues in December 1891. He was the club's first captain in a Cup final, leading the sides out for the 1893 final at Fallowfield against Wolverhampton Wanderers, but returned to Preston later the same year.

Richard Boyle   1894-1896

ANOTHER of Everton's famous Scottish imports, Richard Boyle came to Everton in 1890 and within four years was appointed club captain. A sturdy half-back who led by example, he was strong in the tackle and renowned for his ability to deliver a pinpoint pass over any distance.

There was said to be no more stirring a sight than Boyle robbing a forward and then proceeding to canter half the length of the field before releasing one of his own frontmen with a simple, yet incisive pass. He was also one of the first defenders to specialise in taking free-kicks in and around goal, with several of his eight goals coming from deadball setpieces.

Johnny Holt, the club's first England international

Billy Stewart 1896-1897

STEWART was a footballing innovator, renowned for his exceptionally long throw-in.

In fact so successful and so damaging were his guided missiles launched into opposition penalty areas, that his running and jumping technique before releasing the ball was eventually outlawed.

One third of a famous Everton half-back line which included Holt and Campbell, he played left-half in the 1897 FA Cup final.

Perhaps underlining that camaraderie amongst players is not that much different now to more than a century ago, with Stewart the victim of a practical joke when the Everton team were training at Hoylake.

As he slept, string was attached to every piece of bedroom furniture; then out in the hotel corridor the rest of the team pulled on the strings as hard as they could.

Stewart woke up with the biggest fright of his life!

He made 137 appearances in four years for the Toffees, before joining Bristol City.

An illustration of Jimmy Settle, a bargain £400 buy

THIS FINE SETTLE WAS OBTAINED BY EVERTON FOR £400

Jack Taylor 1898-1900 1905-1908

JACK Taylor's name is never one of the first mentioned when any roll-call of Everton Greats is listed, but his achievements are indisputable.

Only five men have made more appearances for the club - only the great Neville Southall appeared in more FA Cup finals - and it was his pass which eventually led to Sandy Young's winner in the 1906 Cup final.

Taylor moved to Goodison after playing for Dumbarton Athletic and St Mirren. Extremely versatile, the Scotsman began as a centre-forward, moving to the right-wing and then back into defence.

His career was brought to a premature end in the 1910 FA Cup semi-final against Barnsley when a powerful shot struck him in the throat and caused severe damage to his larynx. He had played 456 matches for the club, scoring 80 goals over more than a decade's stalwart service. He died aged 77 after a motoring accident in West Kirby in 1949.

Jimmy Settle 1900-1901

AN instinctive finisher, the Lancastrian from Millom, near Bolton captained Everton during the 1900-01 season when he was just 24 and went on to have a nine-year association with the Blues.

Settle won six England caps between 1899 and 1903, represented the Football League and starred in the 1906 and 1907 FA Cup finals. His goals-per-game ratio was better than a goal every three games before he left for Stockport County in 1908.

Tom Booth 1901-1904

AN Everton stalwart in the days when the last century was in its infancy, Booth was desperately unlucky to miss both the 1906 and 1907 Cup finals. Sidelined through injury when Everton first claimed the Cup at Crystal Palace, he missed out again 12 months later.

He joined Everton from Blackburn Rovers and continued to live in Manchester, but no-one ever doubted his commitment to the Goodison cause.

When Everton met Manchester City in a vital end-of-season clash in 1905, Booth and his namesake Frank were both cautioned in what became an infamous off-the-ball incident. He left Everton for Preston in 1908.

Only six men have made
more appearances for
Everton than Jack Taylor

'His career was brought to a premature end in the 1910 FA Cup
semi-final against Barnsley when a powerful shot struck him in the
throat and caused severe damage to his larynx. He had played 456
matches for the club, scoring 80 goals over more than a decade'

John Moores shakes hands
with Jack Sharp Jnr

William Balmer   1904-1905

THE Balmer brothers represented Everton with
consistency and reliability for almost 15 years.

Robert Balmer made 188 appearances between 1902
and 1912, while older brother Bill made his debut in the
1897-98 campaign and made 331 appearances until
leaving to join Croydon Common of the Southern League
in 1908. William Balmer, to give him his full title,
captained the Blues between 1904 and 1905, the
campaign which saw Everton finish runners-up in the
First Division.

Capped once by England, he also saw nephew Jack
play a couple of times for Everton before World War Two
as the Balmer name continued to represent Everton with
pride.

Jack Sharp   1908-1910

FEATURED elsewhere in this book, Jack Sharp was an
all-rounder who was voted Everton's Millennium Giant for
1900-09. He was already a prosperous businessman
when he retired in 1910, apparently influenced by Jack
Taylor's tragic accident in the 1910 FA Cup semi-final.
However, his cricket career continued for many years. In
1909 he won his three caps for the England Test team,
scoring 105 at The Oval against Australia, the only home

player to score a century in that Ashes series.

Sharp was appointed Lancashire's captain in 1923, aged
45, and continued in that role for two years. He became
the first former professional to serve on England's cricket
selection committee in 1924, a year after he joined the
Everton board.

'A bright and cheerful man who loved a joke', according
to *The Cricketer* magazine, Sharp achieved career figures
of 22,715 first-class runs, averaging 31.11 per innings,
scoring 38 centuries with a highest score of 211. His
wicket haul was 441 at an average of 27.41 runs conceded
per wicket.

The figures are impressive in any era. As a comparison,
Andrew Flintoff's current first-class batting average is
34.90, while his bowling average is 31.82 (at the end of
September 2007).

Sharp's main business interest was his much-loved
eponymous sports store in Whitechapel. It opened in
1903 and the name did not disappear from Liverpool city
centre until the 1990s (the Jack Sharp Sports logo
appeared on the back of the Everton programme for
many seasons in the 1980s).

The company had been taken over by JJB Sports in
1988 and that provides an Everton link in itself as the
organisation is the club's current official retail partner.

Jack Sharp died from bronchitis 1938, aged 59, but
the name lived on at Everton as his son, also called Jack,
spent 33 years on the board, including two as club
chairman from 1965.

Harry Makepeace 1910-1911

LIKE his contemporary Jack Sharp, Harry Makepeace combined successful careers in football and cricket.

Born in Middlesbrough in 1882, Makepeace's family moved to Liverpool when he was 10, attending Queens Road school in the city.

He played for Everton from 1903-14, featuring in the successful 1906 FA Cup final and made 336 appearances, and for Lancashire from 1906-30.

A forward who developed into a fearsome half-back, he went on to coach Everton from 1922-25.

He appeared four times for England at football and cricket, but probably was most distinguished at the latter sport. He remains the oldest player to score a maiden Test century after hitting 117 against Australia in Melbourne in 1920-21 when he was in his 40th year. He scored 44 first-class centuries in total.

A *Liverpool Echo* report of 1920 commented: 'Makepeace has ever appealed to sportsmen by reason of his modesty and his gentlemanliness.

'Success in football and cricket was due to coaching from his father and a determination to rise to the top wrung by persistent practice.'

He coached and advised at Lancs until 1951 and raised money for charity in his latter years, as well as making Christmas parcels for the poor.

A former Lancs and England fast bowler, Roy Tattersall, said of him: "Old 'Shake' was a modest, fatherly figure, always on hand with good advice and praise if deserved.

"He made sure you appeared well turned out and smart on and off the field. 'Take pride in yourself' was one of his sayings."

Makepeace died, aged 70, in Bebington in 1952.

John Maconnachie 1911-1914

EVERTONIANS adored Maconnachie's cool, authoritative approach to the game and he seldom seemed ruffled, often playing his way out of tight situations in his own penalty area.

One of the more skilful defenders, in an age when the full-back's main function was to punt the ball as far downfield as possible, the Scot joined Everton from Hibernian in 1907.

An ever present in 1908-09, he was made captain in 1911 and continued to lead the side up until the outbreak of War.

He recontinued his career at the club after hostilities ceased and ended with 270 Everton appearances – a figure which would undoubtedly have been much greater but for the Great War.

All-round sportsman:
Harry Makepeace

'Makepeace has ever appealed to sportsmen by reason of his modesty and gentlemanliness. Success in football and cricket was due to coaching from his father and a determination to rise to the top wrung by persistent practice'

Jimmy Galt 1914-1915

GALT was the classic example of a footballer whose career was wrecked by War.

Club captain in 1914-15, he led the Blues to the League Championship and the semi-finals of the FA Cup.

But he found that the route to even greater triumphs had been barred by events in Europe and his Everton career ended before it had barely started.

After winning Scottish league championship medals at Glasgow Rangers between 1911 and 1913 and two Scottish caps in 1908, he looked set to become one of the most decorated Anglo-Scottish footballers of his era, until war was declared.

John McDonald 1921-1922

SIGNED from Airdrie in 1920, John McDonald went straight into the side at the start of the 1920-21 season and was appointed club captain in August 1921.

His inspiration was vital to the club as Everton battled against relegation throughout a difficult campaign. A telling influence in the dressing room, it was not his fault that his time at the club coincided with one of the less successful periods in the club's history. By the time the League title next came to Goodison, in 1928, he was playing at New Brighton in the Third Division North.

'A telling influence in the dressing room, it was not his fault that his time at the club coincided with one of the less successful periods in the club's history. By the time the League title next came to Goodison, in 1928, he was playing at New Brighton in the Third Division North'

Jimmy Galt (left) and Hunter Hart

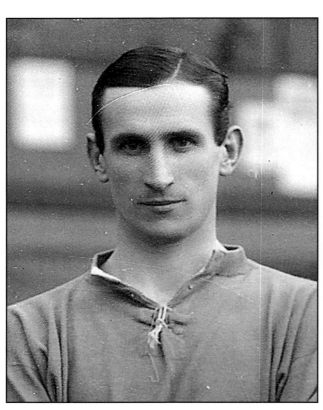

Warney Cresswell, in action (centre)

Hunter Hart   1923-1927
1928-1930

HART, who lost an eye in a childhood accident, played over 300 games for Everton and experienced numerous highs and lows during his Goodison career.

He made his debut during the 1921-22 campaign and was appointed club captain in 1925-26.

His natural leadership qualities were recognised by the club even after he hung up his boots and when he retired in 1930 he joined the Goodison office staff and was appointed assistant secretary in 1936.

Warney Cresswell 1927-1929

ONE of the most talented full-backs to play for Everton, Warney Cresswell - or Warneford, to give him his full title - was captain of the Blues between 1927 and 1929.

Born in South Shields, he started playing football at Stanhope Road School and went on to play as a guest for Hearts and Hibernian during the First World War before joining his hometown team.

'Hart, who lost an eye in a childhood accident, played over 300 games for Everton ... his natural leadership qualities were recognised after he hung up his boots'

A classy defender, he stood out for his pose and calmness.

Unlike many defenders of his day, he was able to resist the temptation of throwing himself into full-blooded tackles, preferring a more measured approach which enabled him to make many a timely interception.

His consistent displays caught the eye of nearby Sunderland and, at the age of 24, he moved to Roker Park for a fee of £5,500.

He moved on to Goodison in February 1927 and embarked on a successful spell which saw him win Division One championships in 1928 and 1932 and a Division Two title in 1931.

He also won an FA Cup winner's medal in 1933. He was capped seven times by England at senior level between 1921 and 1929, having also won international honours as a schoolboy. He made history by becoming the first player to make 500 Football League appearances after the First World War.

Surprisingly, he only scored one goal for the club and that came in a 4-2 home defeat at the hands of Manchester United in April 1929.

He had a two-year stint as club captain, succeeding Hunter Hart who resumed as skipper in 1929. Cresswell's spell as captain gave him the unique pleasure of leading the side in the season Dixie Dean achieved his astonishing feat of scoring 60 goals in a season as Everton won the league.

He played his final game for the Blues against Bolton Wanderers in September 1935.

After leaving Everton, he moved into management and had spells in charge of Port Vale, Northampton Town and Dartford before moving into the pub trade and he was a licensee for many years.

He died in a South Shields hospital in October 1973 at the age of 75.

A George Green cartoon of Warney Cresswell that appeared in the Echo at that time

'Unlike many defenders of his day, he was able to resist the temptation of throwing himself into full-blooded tackles, preferring a more measured approach which enabled him to make many a timely interception'

Ben Williams 1930-1931

BEN Williams was the man who led Everton back into the First Division in 1930-31. A talented boxer, he actually considered a career in the ring before turning to football and formed a formidable partnership with Warney Cresswell.

He was capped 10 times by Wales, but in January 1933 suffered an injury which required a cartilage operation and he never fully recovered.

Dixie Dean 1931-1937

THE club's most celebrated star, Everton's greatest goalscorer and the Toffees' first No. 9, Dixie Dean was also the first captain to lead the club out at Wembley, for the 1933 FA Cup final.

That came in the middle of his spell as captain, a period which also saw him lead the 1931-32 title winners and play some of the finest football of his career.

Jock Thomson 1937-1939

BORN in Renfrewshire, Scotland, Thomson was a left-half who gained three championship medals with Everton – the first a Second Division title in 1930-31, followed by a Division One crown in 1931-32 – and another in 1938-39 when he captained the club to the title. He was also a member of the 1933 FA Cup-winning team.

An aggressive six-footer, he had played junior football in Scotland before signing for Dundee, moving to Merseyside almost five years later.

His only full season as captain saw him lead the Blues to that memorable title triumph, but it was to be his final campaign with the club, retiring in December 1939 although he went on to make guest appearances during the Second World War for Aldershot, Fulham and Carnoustie.

After the War, he had a three-year spell as manager of Manchester City before moving back north of the border to Carnoustie, where he became a pub landlord until 1974. He died in the town in 1979.

Norman Greenhalgh 1946-1949

A MODEL of footballing consistency and an ever-present player in Everton's championship-winning campaign of 1938-39, Norman Greenhalgh wore the armband for the Blues upon the resumption of league football after World War Two.

Peter Farrell was introduced to the side during that 1946-47 season and was groomed for the captaincy, but Greenhalgh led the Blues before leaving on a free transfer at the age of 34 in May 1949.

After failing to make the grade with his hometown club Bolton, Greenhalgh made his mark in league football with New Brighton, being snapped up by Everton for £800 in January 1938, forming a fine full-back partnership with Billy Cook.

He was admired by no less a winger than Stanley Matthews, who appreciated his rugged, confident approach.

Although he never played for England in a recognised full international, he did represent his country in a War-time fixture against Scotland.

But for the hostilities, Greenhalgh would almost certainly have made many more league appearances for the Blues.

His only league goal for the club came in a 4-0 home defeat of Leicester City in March 1939 as Everton closed in on the title.

After retiring from football, he became a licensee. He died in 1995.

T.G. Jones 1948-1949

THE Welsh maestro's enormous contribution to the People's Club is detailed elsewhere in this book, but his spell as club captain came during the 1948-49 season, while young Irishman Peter Farrell was being fully groomed for the role.

In January 1950 Everton agreed to his release after a career which also saw him win 17 caps for Wales and 11 in War-time internationals.

He returned to North Wales to become player-manager of Pwllheli and District. He also ran a hotel then took over as manager of Bangor City in 1956 and enjoyed an 11-year stint in charge of the Farrar Road club. In 1962, he was in charge of the North Walians when they took on Napoli in the European Cup Winners' Cup after guiding City to the Welsh Cup the previous season. Jones's men defeated the Italians 2-0 in the home leg but lost 3-1 in Italy. With no away-goal rule, a replay took place but Bangor again lost 3-1. After a season in charge of Rhyl, "T.G." turned his hand to journalism and became a football writer for the North Wales edition of the *Daily Post*. He later also ran a newsagents in Bangor.

He was elected as a Millennium Giant by Everton in 2000, one of the first 11 from the club's long history to be so honoured, which speaks volumes for the esteem in which he was held.

T.G. Jones died on January 3, 2004, aged 86.

Footballer turned journalist: T.G. Jones

Irish skipper was adored by the fans

Peter Farrell   1949-1957

ONE of the most popular players to represent the Blues, Farrell joined Everton from Shamrock Rovers in a £10,000 deal in August 1946 which also saw his close friend Tommy Eglington make the switch to Goodison.

A right-half, Farrell was groomed as captain from the start, became adored by Evertonians and currently stands eighth in the club's all-time list of appearance makers.

Born in Dalkey, near Dublin in August 1923, he played his first schoolboy match for Cabinteely United Boys at the age of 13, going on to sign for Shamrock Rovers as an amateur in July 1939, turning professional on his 17th birthday the following year.

He was one of a handful of players to appear in full internationals for both Northern Ireland and the Republic of Ireland. He represented Northern Ireland on seven occasions when they were able to select players born in the Republic for the Home International Championship. He won the first two of his 28 caps for the Republic of Ireland after the Second World War when he was still playing for Shamrock Rovers, just months before his move to Everton. In 1949 he helped to make history when he scored one of the goals for the Republic against England at Goodison Park as Ireland became the first non-British team to defeat England at home.

He soon became a favourite at Goodison and was appointed captain in 1948-49, being temporarily replaced by T.G. Jones in 1949-50 before regaining the armband in 1950-51 and leading the club almost continuously before his departure to Tranmere Rovers.

One of the many highlights during his time with the Blues was leading the club back to Division One as runners-up in the 1953-54 season. He also led the Blues to the semi-final of the FA Cup in 1953.

He told the *Liverpool Echo*: "Had anybody told me when I first joined Everton that I should have the pleasure and privilege of leading them as captain, and, better still, helping the club to regain its First Division status, I'm afraid I should have been a little sceptical."

But after leading the Blues back to the top flight,

Farrell was quick to pay tribute to those around him.

"You can take it from me that no captain could have the honour of being skipper to a better crowd of lads. We were all pals both on and off the field."

The *Liverpool Echo* paid tribute to Farrell following the Blues' return to the top flight.

"With Farrell as leader Everton will set a lively pace among the elite next term! This burly Irishman, a 90-minute player if ever there was one, has done much to inspire his men to their triumphs. By personal example he has shown the way, and if over-eagerness in the cause of his club has sometimes put him on the wrong path, he is the first to try and remedy matters. Farrell has been worth over and over again the small fee paid to Shamrock Rovers."

He became player-manager of Tranmere in October 1957 and finally called time on a fine career following the Blues' 5-2 Liverpool Senior Cup win over Rovers at Goodison in May 1960.

After Everton skipper Tom Jones had received the trophy, Farrell thanked everyone and wished Everton well in the future, explaining that he had 'come to the end of the road.'

Following spells as manager of Sligo Rovers in Ireland and North Wales side Holywell Town, he made a brief playing comeback with Drogheda in 1963 and returned to Dublin to run his own insurance business. One of Everton's best-loved servants, he died in 2001.

T.E. Jones   1957-1961

THOMAS Edwin Jones was a one-club man who served Everton with distinction having joined them as a schoolboy.

A product of the local schoolboy system, his leadership qualities first came to the fore when he captained the Liverpool County FA youth team and later the England schools team.

The Liverpool-born defender toured Ghana and Nigeria during the summer of 1958 and captained an England XI against the British Army.

Originally a right full-back, Jones had officially joined

Everton on May 10, 1945 and went into the Colts team alongside George Rankin and they established themselves as a full-back partnership.

He worked his way up through Everton's junior teams and in the 1948-49 season, manager Cliff Britton recognised in him the potential to be a centre-half. Such a view was vindicated as the youngster turned in a series of consistent performances in the Central League team.

He was eventually handed a debut at Arsenal on September 6, 1950 and although Everton lost 2-1, Jones made an accomplished start to his long career in the senior side. So much so that Leslie Edwards' match report in the *Liverpool Echo* was headlined: 'Everton Lose Match: Find Centre-Half'.

'That final win at Oldham was a highlight of my Goodison days, Had it been 6-0, we would have won the title, but that did not really matter. We were back in Division One and it was a great feeling'

Everton were captained during this period by Peter Farrell and, like his skipper, Jones was a true gentleman who went about his business efficiently.

The Blues were relegated in 1951 but Jones would later point to the promotion back to Division One in 1954 as the highlight of his Everton career.

"That final win at Oldham was a highlight of my Goodison days. Had it been 6-0, we would have won the title, but that did not really matter.

"We were back in Division One and it was a great feeling."

He was a natural choice to take over the armband from Farrell in 1957, leading the Blues for four seasons, with the Blues finishing fourth in 1960-61.

He was likened to his namesake, T.G. Jones, with an *Echo* tribute to mark his 250th league game for the club, in 1956, commenting: 'He relies purely on skill and football artistry, allied to his excellent sense of positioning to see him through the toughest of games.

'Though quite strongly built, he rarely calls on his physical attributes. When he does, they are utilised with the same scrupulous fairness that characterises all his play.

'Considering his consistency over the past few seasons, Jones has been unfortunate not to gain top representative honours.'

One of the best players never to win a full England cap, the excellence of Billy Wright was the main reason why he didn't add to his England youth honours.

After more than 400 appearances and 14 goals (he was Everton's penalty taker at one stage), he briefly played non-League football for Burscough and Chorley before coaching in Canada for the Montral Italia club.

He returned to the club's coaching staff, overseeing the club's youngsters and later scouted for managers from Harry Catterick to Howard Kendall.

He went on to work for Littlewoods, completing 30 years' service before his retirement.

Still living on Merseyside, "T.E.", now 75, still watches the occasional match at Goodison.

'There's Denis Law, Jimmy Greaves and me'

Roy Vernon 1961-1965

A WELSH inside-forward, Vernon was a silken dart of a player who showed maturity beyond his years.

He was lured to Goodison Park from Blackburn in February 1960 and within a year had been appointed club captain.

In the mid 60s he was asked to name the most talented goalscorers of his day. "There's Denis Law", he replied, "there's Jimmy Greaves and there's me."

His answer owed nothing to misplaced arrogance, but more to a natural, colossal self confidence which totally befitted his abilities as a player.

He forged a compelling partnership in the Everton forward line with Alex Young, one all shimmering, artistic touches, the other a rapier-like finisher.

He headed the club's goalcharts in each of his four full seasons on Merseyside, including leading the side to the 1962-63 league title when he clinched the championship with a hat-trick in the final match of the season against Fulham.

No stranger to controversy, he had already fallen foul of strict disciplinarian Harry Catterick several times when the opportunity came to join Stoke in March 1965.

All parties concerned were happy to do a deal, but Roy Vernon was sorely missed by his fans at Goodison who appreciated a player who also proved one of the most reliable penalty takers in the club's history...missing just once.

'Labby will always be known as the captain of Everton'

Brian Labone   1965-1971

THE untimely death of one of Everton's greatest leaders in April 2006 is still felt keenly around the People's Club.

The archetypal gentle giant, Labone's passion for Everton coursed through his veins and the sense of pride he felt when Harry Catterick handed him the captain's armband couldn't have been more evident. His love of the Blues remained as strong as ever to his dying day.

Labby joined Everton on leaving school and came through the ranks to turn professional in July 1957, going on to become one of the Blues' greatest servants in a 15-year spell at the club which saw him make more than 530 appearances.

A dominant defender who was assured on the ground and commanding in the air, the local lad led by example and was the ideal skipper in every way.

Labby had already won a league championship in 1962-63 and later captained the side to another title triumph in 1970.

Yet of all the successes, the one which stood out most was climbing the famous Wembley steps to receive the 1966 FA Cup from Princess Margaret.

"We'd been down 2-0 and won 3-2. It flashed past but it was fantastic," he said. "You only had one chance. In the league you could have a couple of bad days and still win it, but lose in the Cup and you were out."

Labby may have added a World Cup winners' medal to his roll of honour a few months later but famously withdrew from the England reckoning as he prepared for his summer marriage.

He did play in the 1970 finals in Mexico however and was capped 26 times by his country.

After eventually retiring in June 1972, he continued to serve the club with distinction in various capacities, latterly as a matchday meeter and greeter where his gregarious nature made him a firm favourite with all who had the privilege of coming into contact with him.

Everton are fortunate to have had many great men lead them and the words of another, Kevin Ratcliffe, summed up Labby's contribution to the club perfectly.

"Brian was Everton. If you could put together a team of every player that has ever captained Everton, every one of us would turn to Brian to lead us out. He will always be known as the captain of Everton."

Alan Ball   1971

HE only wore the armband for a matter of months but Alan Ball remains extremely proud to have been an Everton skipper.

Ball took over when an Achilles tendon injury forced Brian Labone into a premature retirement in August 1971. By Christmas of that year Harry Catterick had sold the World Cup-winning midfielder to Arsenal.

During that short spell Ball attempted to lead by example, and it was an example he learnt from his predecessor, the great Labone.

"I felt pride, wonderful pride, when I was captain," he said. "It was an honour to take over from Labby. Anybody who has ever captained a big club, which Everton are, will tell you it's a great honour. I tried my best but I could never replace Brian because he was Everton from being a kid all the way through. I came when I was young but I started at another football club."

Ball was only 21 when he signed for Everton in the summer of 1966, immediately after the World Cup. Even in the 21st century, Ball was almost in awe of the unassuming but unquestioned authority Labone exuded.

"I was under as good a captain as you'll ever know in Brian Labone. He didn't just toss the coin up – he did everything.

"He made sure you were aware of your responsibilities to the club. He didn't tell you twice; once he'd asked you to go and do something, you did it.

"Every time we went down to London and we travelled by train, you had to meet at a particular Chinese restaurant and we all ate together as a group. I never realised how important team spirit is. Labby was very, very aware of that and I tried to take that on.

"He kept everybody in line, he never let anybody get carried away with anything. I was a cocky little devil, I was arrogant and I was flying at the time but he made sure I was aware of my responsibilities.

"I'd like to think I was also a real team player. He made me aware that that is what's needed."

Giants of England: Bally and Bobby Moore

'I felt wonderful pride, when I was captain. It was an honour to take over from Labby'

Sand men: Howard Kendall
and team-mates are put
through their paces during
pre-season training

Howard Kendall   1972-1974

HOWARD Kendall was an obvious choice as captain when Alan Ball was sold to Arsenal. He went on to show his leadership qualities even more decisively a decade later, when he was appointed manager.

Kendall had been at the club five years when he was handed the captain's armband and was a hugely respected figure, not to mention a very talented midfielder.

It is still one of the great mysteries of modern football why he was never capped by his country.

A member of one of the most influential midfield combinations the club has ever known – the revered Ball-Harvey-Kendall triumvirate – it was only Everton's pressing need for a quality goalscorer which convinced Billy Bingham to let him leave the club in 1974.

Everton had agreed a British record transfer fee with Birmingham City for Bob Latchford, but Birmingham also demanded Howard Kendall as part of the transaction.

The Blues reluctantly agreed, but it wouldn't be long before Kendall was back at Goodison, delighting Evertonians once again.

'Kendall was an obvious choice as captain when Alan Ball was sold to Arsenal. He went on to show his leadership qualities even more decisively a decade later, when he was appointed manager'

Roger Kenyon   1974-1976

A speedy and reliable centre-half, Kenyon made more than 300 appearances for Everton, after being handed the unenviable task of following Brian Labone into the heart of the Toffees' defence.

He was a substitute, but wasn't called upon, in the 1968 FA Cup final, but was needed during the 1969-70 Championship-winning campaign – sadly, not quite enough to qualify for a medal.

He forced his way into the regular starting line-up the following season and by the mid-70s was a regular and influential member of the Blues' back-four.

Appointed skipper in 1974, a car accident interrupted his progress, but he was still called into a number of England squads without ever making it across the white line to collect a full cap.

He stayed at Everton for almost 15 years before moving to the west coast of Canada and Vancouver Whitecaps.

In 1979 he ended his career the way he started it, helping his team to a league title.

'The "Lyons for England" chants from the Gwladys Street never came true'

THE truest of True Blues, it was often said that if you cut Mick Lyons, he would bleed blue blood – and his appointment as club captain was one of the least controversial decisions in the club's history.

He once readily admitted he would run through a brick wall to further the Everton cause, but for the most part he contented himself with halting opposition forwards in their tracks.

That was his most natural role of centre-half, but he also readily threw his weight into opposition penalty boxes as an emergency striker, contributing 59 goals throughout his 473-match Everton career – and even once as a goalkeeper in the days before substitute keepers were allowed on the bench.

Universally admired, he won England U23 and B caps, although the "Lyons for England" chants which were

Mick Lyons   1976-1982

unfailingly bellowed from the Gwladys Street every time he led the side out, surprisingly never quite came true.

He spent more than a decade at the club, and one of his proudest moments was leading the side out at Wembley for the 1977 League Cup final.

That match finished goalless, and despite a headed equaliser into the Stretford End in the second replay at Old Trafford, Aston Villa were triumphant.

That was as close as Lyons ever got to claiming silverware with his beloved Blues, but Everton and Mick Lyons always seemed made for each other and he returned as a club coach under Colin Harvey in the 1980s.

Billy Wright — 1982

NEPHEW of the much loved Tommy Wright, Billy will be remembered as a classy centre-half who lost his Everton place because he was overweight.

Hours before a league game at Ipswich in December 1982, Howard Kendall told his club captain he was being left out as a disciplinary measure for weighing eight pounds more than the club decreed.

The media headlines were predictable – and "Billy Bunter" never recovered from the shattering blow to his confidence and he moved on to Birmingham City.

Prior to his switch, Wright had made 198 appearances and won England U21 honours, but after his shock omission he saw Mark Higgins and Kevin Ratcliffe forge an impressive partnership and reluctantly had to accept his Everton career was over.

> 'Howard Kendall told his club captain he was being left out for weighing eight pounds more than the club decreed. The media headlines were predictable – and 'Billy Bunter' never recovered from the blow'

Mark Higgins — 1983-1984

BUT for a tragically ill-timed injury, Mark Higgins might well have been the defensive inspiration at the heart of Everton's mid-80s glory days.

A hugely talented defender, Higgins was on the verge of an England call-up when he suffered a crippling hip injury at the age of 26.

He had just helped Everton into the quarter-final of the 1983-84 Milk Cup with a replay victory over West Ham, when he was diagnosed with what was thought to be a simple groin strain.

Sadly it turned out to be a serious pelvic disorder and despite two operations and numerous attempts at a comeback, he was told he would never play again.

Higgins, however, refused to admit defeat. Medical breakthroughs enabled him to recover a measure of fitness and after paying back all of his insurance pay-out he tried again with Manchester United.

The time he had spent out of the game, however, meant that a top-flight return proved beyond him, but he refused to give in and continued to offer commendable service to first Bury and then Stoke City.

It was a spirited retort to the fates which had cruelly robbed him of untold glories at Everton.

Hero Kev's 'inspirational service'

QUITE simply, Kevin Ratcliffe is the most successful captain in the history of Everton Football Club.

He led the club to two League Championships, one FA Cup, the club's only European trophy and provided inspirational service over 493 matches in Royal Blue.

It was his astonishing pace which often attracted most attention, but Ratcliffe was also

Kevin Ratcliffe 1984-1991

quick of thought and read the game with instinctive shrewdness.

Voted as a Millennium Giant, his achievements are chronicled more fully elsewhere in this book, but Ratcliffe, quite simply, is one of Everton's all-time greats.

Dave Watson   1992-1997

ANOTHER to be installed as a Millennium Giant, Watson is the last Everton captain to enjoy the sensation of raising major silverware aloft when he led the Blues to FA Cup glory at Wembley in 1995.

One of only two outfield Evertonians to make more than 500 appearances for the club – and this after a 200-game spell with Norwich City, Watson saw it all during more than a decade-and-a-half at Goodison Park.

He was a title winner in 1987, a caretaker-manager a decade later – and in between enjoyed the odd distinction of becoming the club's oldest European debutant at the age of 33 in 1995.

He succeeded Kevin Ratcliffe as captain in 1992, a decision fully endorsed by his predecessor, and three years later was lifting the FA Cup at Wembley.

That was the highlight of his Everton career, although 12 months earlier, after the remarkable relegation escape against Wimbledon, then director Bill Kenwright bumped into him in the Goodison Park car park and asked why he wasn't getting into his car.

Watson replied: "I'm not taking the car, I'll be doing cartwheels all the way home!"

'Then director Bill Kenwright bumped into him in the Goodison Park car park and asked why he wasn't getting into his car. Watson replied: "I'm not taking the car, I'll be doing cartwheels all the way home!"'

Gary Speed 1997-1998

GARY Speed's appointment as club captain was controversial.

Handed the armband in the dressing room just minutes before the opening match of the 1997-98 season against Crystal Palace, the displaced Dave Watson later said: "Let's just say Howard's timing left a little to be desired."

But that was nothing compared to the controversy generated when Speed fell out with the manager and refused to travel to West Ham just six months later. He was sold to Newcastle United within weeks, a sad end to a dream move for a childhood Evertonian.

Speed had once been the paperboy for the most successful captain in Everton's history, Kevin Ratcliffe. But while Ratcliffe is revered by Evertonians, Speed's departure is filled with recriminations.

Duncan Ferguson 1997-1998 2002-2003

HOWARD Kendall left most seasoned observers, not to mention Evertonians, scratching their heads in concern when he turned to his centre-forward with the dreadful disciplinary record to lead the club in a vital Premiership match against Bolton Wanderers.

Not for the first time, it proved to be an inspired Kendall decision. Ferguson scored the first hat-trick of his career - a trio of stunning headers - and went on to inspire the side to a last-gasp relegation escape.

He scored further crucial goals against Chelsea, Liverpool, Crystal Palace, Barnsley and Leeds United, pushing himself through a painful knee injury to help secure the club's status.

A number of players wore the captain's armband during that troubled campaign - Slaven Bilic and Nick Barmby amongst them - but Ferguson would be handed the captaincy again, this time when David Moyes began as boss four years later.

Once again the reponsibilities of captaincy brought the best out of Ferguson, scoring in each of Moyes' first three games in charge of the Blues.

Don Hutchison 1998-2000

IT was a vindicating moment for Don Hutchison when Walter Smith handed him the captain's armband for a spell during the 1998-99 season.

He had arrived at Goodison as a former Liverpool favourite, not to mention a player with a chequered past, but he re-invented himself as a responsible and reliable midfielder, and was rewarded when Smith handed him the responsibility of leading the side out at West Ham in December 1998.

He kept the armband for several matches, then when Dave Watson's limbs finally failed him in 1999-2000, was given the responsibility of captaincy on a more permanent basis.

It was a brave decision by Smith, but one that Hutchison justified with his effort, commitment and performance levels. Hutchison was voted Everton's Player of the Season by several supporters' groups, before leaving for Sunderland at the end of the season.

Richard Gough 2000

GOUGH was clearly a captain in waiting from the moment he joined the Blues in the summer of 1999. His first experience as skipper was a sobering one - a 5-1 humbling at Old Trafford - but he finished the season with the armband in his sole possession.

Gough was Everton's oldest post-War outfield player - he made his debut aged 39 years and 24 days - so his tenure as skipper was always destined to be short-lived, but he performed the duties admirably until a knee injury finally brought the curtain down on a honourable career.

Richard Gough combined experience with top quality

Kevin Campbell 2001-2002

FEW players have made as instant an impact at Everton as "Super" Kevin Campbell, the striker who arrived on-loan from Trabzonspor in March 1999 – and ended top scorer eight matches later!

Campbell's goal blitz at the end of the 1998-99 season hauled Everton away from the heart of a relegation dogfight – and created a clamour for his permanent transfer which Walter Smith couldn't ignore.

He completed a £3m move and quickly became one of the most respected players in the squad.

When Walter Smith made him club captain in 2001, he spoke of his pride at becoming the first black skipper of Everton – and for a spell his strike partnership with Francis Jeffers looked richly promising.

Sadly both were stricken down by injuries, but despite Campbell's own long-term injury problems in each of the 1999-2000, 2000-01 and 2001-02 seasons, he still managed to rack up 25 goals in 67 starts.

'Playing for the club of my dreams'

Alan Stubbs   2003-2005

"IF I sign for Everton I'll be playing for the club of my dreams," said boyhood Blue Alan Stubbs while he was negotiating a switch from Celtic in the summer of 2001.

"I've always dreamed of playing for Everton and this is my last chance to do so. I simply cannot wait to pull on an Everton jersey for the first time. I know it is going to be the best feeling I've ever had in football."

That feeling was surpassed when Stubbs was made captain for the first time at the start of the 2003-04 season.

It was a responsibility he carried out with relish and while Kevin Campbell remained club captain, his increasing injury problems meant that Stubbs was effectively the unofficial skipper for the majority of the season.

David Weir   2005-2006

WEIR already enjoyed the status of one of Everton's best value for money buys of all-time and had captained the team many times since his arrival from Hearts in February 1999.

But it wasn't until his career was in its twilight zone that David Moyes finally appointed him as club captain.

Never the most vocal of players, he led by example and his commitment to the cause was never questioned.

He made 269 appearances for Everton, after joining the club at a time when he was already considered to have reached veteran status.

Phil Neville   2007-

LIKE Everton's very first Football League captain almost 120 years earlier, Phil Neville joined Everton from one of their fiercest north-west rivals. But while Nick Ross spent just a single season at Everton then returned to Preston, Neville's switch from Manchester United quickly saw him embrace all aspects of the People's Club.

"They say Everton are the People's Club, and it really is. Everyone mucks in together and there is no better atmosphere," he said.

After a battling 1-0 win over Blackburn Rovers in February 2006, with Everton reduced to 10 men in the opening minutes, he declared: "You wouldn't get an atmosphere in any other ground like you had here at Goodison on Saturday. It was really special.

"The bigger the obstacle, the more the challenge, it brings out the best in Everton. There's always been that never-say-die attitude here."

Neville was clearly suited for the captain's role, and for the 2007-08 season – after numerous trial runs with the armband – he was made club captain.

"Being given the captaincy at Everton so soon – I got it for the Bucharest game – was one of the proudest moments of my career," he declared.

"I have never captained a team for a sustained period of time. It was a great honour.

"I didn't think the transition from Manchester United would be easy but it has been. A big part of that was how the players made me feel so welcome so full credit to the boys and the staff. I'd always been a Red but now I class myself as a Blue and as an Evertonian.

"Somebody asked me the other day if I feel I belong here and I really do feel a part of this club. The fans make you feel a part of it. From the outside looking in, they look good fans but when you actually play for the club, you realise they're a special kind of people and a special kind of football fan.

"I feel like an Evertonian now. They are a special kind of people. When you look from the outside, you hear former managers and players talking about a special kind of fan and you just think, 'oh, all fans are the same.' But these are different; Everton is their lives.

"They don't demand Ronaldinho-skill but, as they put it, if you put in your shift you'll do, win, lose or draw. That impresses me."

'From the outside looking in, they look good fans but when you actually play for the club, you realise they're a special kind of people and a special kind of football fan. I feel like an Evertonian now. They are a special kind of people'

People's Club New Giants

CHAPTER 8

Legends nominated
as Giants since
the Millennium

Everton

'It was with crushing irony that it was Alan Ball's heart which gave out first'

HIS exclusion from the original list of Everton Giants caused the greatest debate. So there was never any argument that Alan Ball would be the first name added to the Hall of Fame when it was extended in 2001.

It says much for the quality of the competition in the first place that "The Golden Vision" kept the flame-haired firebrand out of the vote for the 1960s' Giant – because in many fans' eyes, the midfield maestro is second only to Dixie Dean in the all-time list of Everton legends.

So it is strange to consider that the greatest achievement of Alan Ball's football life came just days before he signed for Everton Football Club.

July 30, 1966 is the most significant day in English football history, the afternoon Alf Ramsey's wingless wonders claimed the World Cup. One of the more enduring images of that never to be forgotten day is of a 21-year-old from Farnworth tirelessly covering every blade of the Wembley grass for his country's cause. Alan Ball was the youngest member of Ramsey's team, and watching smugly from the sidelines was Harry Catterick. The Blues' boss knew he had a British record fee of £110,000 lined up for the midfield inspiration – and not a single penny of it was ever begrudged.

Ball scored on his debut at Fulham, a match-winning strike, but it was seven days later that his love affair with the Evertonians really ignited. Just a fortnight after Everton had been comprehensively outplayed in a FA Charity Shield match by their Mersey neighbours, without Ball in their line-up, they met again, this time with Alan Ball pulling the strings.

More than 64,000 spectators crammed into Goodison Park to see Everton win 3-1, with Ball scoring twice. It would be a trademark moment he repeated many times throughout his career. Later that season he was the scourge of Liverpool once again when over 100,000 fans saw him claim the only goal of an FA Cup fifth-round tie.

Over 60,000 watched the game at Goodison Park, while another 40,000 watched the 'live' screening at Anfield. His goals return for a midfielder was prodigious, but it wasn't just his ability to finish which was admired by Evertonians. He was tigerish in the tackle, could pass the ball quite beautifully, was as brave as a lion and, of course, had limitless stamina. His peak was possibly the

Millennium Giant   2001

period between 1967 and 1969, but in the 1969-70 season he was the inspiration behind a stunning title charge.

Alongside Howard Kendall and Colin Harvey, Ball formed the most revered midfield triumvirate in the club's history. Everton stormed to the title with second-placed Leeds United nine points adrift (in the days when only two points were awarded for a win). That the Blues didn't dominate the decade rankled with Ball. Although he didn't want to leave, there was widespread disbelief amongst Evertonians when he was sold to Arsenal in December 1971. His departure was mourned like no other before him and arguably, no other since. The fans knew he was irreplaceable and they saw another British record fee of £220,000 as no consolation.

A total of 251 appearances yielded a highly impressive 79 goals, 39 of his 72 England caps were collected whilst an Everton player and those who still insist that his exit was premature can point to the fact that he went on to play a further 400 matches after leaving Goodison.

Undoubtedly one of the finest players to ever wear the Royal Blue jersey, Alan Ball was a unique footballing package. The infectious enthusiasm, the sublime skill, the boundless energy, the goalscoring knack, the sheer consistency, the flame-coloured hair, the high-pitched voice and the white boots – the man is an Everton legend and was an entirely appropriate choice as the first Everton Giant of the 21st century.

It was with crushing irony that it should be Alan Ball's heart which gave out first, at the inordinately early age of 61. A ceaseless study in perpetual motion – Ball was famed for his energy, his passion and his refusal to quit any battle, no matter how hopeless the odds.

But almost a year on from the day the Blues lost the "Last of the Corinthians", Brian Labone, Ball collapsed with a heart attack tending to a fire in the back garden of his Hampshire home, and died.

His legacy, however, will never be forgotten.

ALAN BALL FACTFILE

Born: Farnworth, 1945
Everton Appearances: 251
Everton Goals: 79
Everton Honours: First Division
Championship winner 1969-70
FA Cup runner-up 1968
FA Charity Shield 1970
England caps: 72 (39 with Everton)
World Cup winner 1966
Awarded MBE 2000

'There are many Evertonians who can claim to be legends, few can claim to be unique'

RAY Wilson is one of the few Everton Giants who the term 'world class' can be genuinely placed alongside.

The evidence was produced on July 30, 1966, when Ray Wilson and 10 of his England colleagues defeated West Germany in a football match at Wembley to turn themselves into national treasures and bring the World Cup to these shores for the one and only time.

Many Evertonians can lay claim to being a legend, but few can be labelled as unique, which is why Ray Wilson was named the Everton Giant for 2002.

His love affair with Everton was a late developer.

Wilson was actually 29 years of age when Harry Catterick finally secured his signature in 1964.

"Everton was a far bigger club than Huddersfield," he later explained.

"I was 13 years at Huddersfield, and most of that time was spent in the Second Division. I did try to get away a few times, but they wouldn't let me. I was 29 when Harry finally got me for Everton and I think Huddersfield realised that it would be daft not to sell me at that age.

"I was a bit annoyed in a sense, because I would have liked to have moved in my mid-twenties. It didn't affect my international career, thankfully, because there were a few of us at either Second Division clubs or with average First Division clubs. George Cohen and Johnny Haynes were at Fulham, Jimmy Armfield was at Blackpool and that's the way it was."

The irony is, Everton could well have snapped up Wilson 14 years earlier!

"I had a trial with Huddersfield as a kid and there was an Everton scout watching me," he revealed. "I got a letter from Everton offering me a deal, but I felt loyal to Huddersfield. But I remember looking around Goodison properly for the first time after I'd joined and I thought to myself, 'my word, what have I been missing out on all these years? I should have been here years ago.'"

Ray put pen-to-paper in the summer of 1964, two years before his memorable year.

Not only did he win the World Cup, but he was also a part of the Everton team that won one of the most dramatic FA Cup finals of all time, coming from two goals down to triumph 3-2 over Sheffield Wednesday.

Ray had sole ownership of the left-back jersey for both

club and country and his reputation as a defender of extremely rare quality was worldwide, but injury prevented him from playing a part in the magnificent Championship side that Harry Catterick fashioned just four years later.

By the time The Toffees lifted the league crown, Ray had moved to Oldham Athletic.

"Strangely enough, Everton won the league just before I joined them and then they won it again just after I left ... which I hope was just a coincidence!" he joked.

In later years, after his career had run its course, he shunned the typical trades that footballers of his era often pursued. Instead, he built a successful undertaker's business in Huddersfield.

Wilson and four of his 1966 team-mates - Hunt, George Cohen, Nobby Stiles and Alan Ball - were awarded the MBE for services to football in 2000 after a high-profile campaign conducted by sections of the media.

RAY WILSON FACTFILE

Born: Shirebrook, Derbyshire 1934
Everton Appearances: 154
Everton Goals: 0
Everton Honours: FA Cup winner 1966, runner-up 1968
England caps: 63
World Cup winner 1966

'His elevation to the status of Everton Giant was the equivalent of a golfing shoo-in'

BY the relatively tender age of 24, Kevin Ratcliffe had already become the most successful captain in Everton history.

His achievement in leading the Blues to FA Cup, European Cup Winners' Cup, FA Charity Shield and League Championship glory gave him his place in the pantheon of fame. But he confirmed that status by captaining another league title-winning team in 1987.

Such was Everton's level of dominance in the domestic game under his leadership that he led the club out at Wembley Stadium no fewer than 12 times – in four FA Cup finals, one Milk Cup final, four FA Charity Shields, a Simod Cup final, a Zenith Data Systems Cup final and the Football League's invitational Centenary Tournament in 1988.

His elevation to the status of Everton Giant in 2003 was the equivalent of a golfing shoo-in.

Ratcliffe's natural leadership qualities played a prominent part in his rise to Goodison glory. So, too, did burning acceleration, an immaculate reading of the game, a tough and uncompromising attitude – and a hugely under-rated left foot.

It is often overlooked that on the days Kevin Sheedy was injured or unavailable, Ratcliffe would be entrusted with free-kick duties around the periphery of opposition penalty boxes.

However, his goals record at Everton was the only modest tally of his entire career.

He scored just twice, both away from Goodison Park – and the last, famously, at Anfield.

That came in the spring of 1986, almost a decade after Everton had taken him on as a young apprentice.

He made his debut as a 19-year-old against Manchester United at Old Trafford, successfully shackling Joe Jordan, but his first-team appearances after that were sporadic and often at left-back.

His inability to hold down a place in his favoured central defensive role led to early run-ins with Gordon Lee and Howard Kendall, but when he eventually displaced Billy Wright in 1982, there was no looking back.

He was appointed club captain in December 1983 and three months later took over the same role with his

Millennium Giant   2003

country.

He ended his Everton career just a handful of games short of 500 – Brian Labone was the only other outfield player to top that figure – and he was granted a well-earned testimonial match in 1989.

He eventually severed his Everton links in the spring of 1992, but his place in any Goodison Hall of Fame had long since been assured.

He concluded his playing career with spells at Dundee, Cardiff City, Nottingham Forest, Derby County and Chester City.

Then as a manager he was responsible for one of the more embarrassing moments of recent Everton history, when his Shrewsbury Town minnows knocked David Moyes' Premiership side out of the FA Cup.

Predictably, Ratcliffe took little joy from the occasion.

KEVIN RATCLIFFE FACTFILE

Born: Mancot, 1960
Everton Appearances: 493
Everton Goals: 2
Everton Honours: First Division Championship winner 1984-85, 1986-87, runner-up 1985-86
FA Cup winner 1984, runner-up 1985, 1986, 1989
European Cup Winners' Cup winner 1984-85
League Cup runner-up 1983-84
FA Charity Shield winner 1984, 1985, 1986 (shared), 1987
Simod Cup runner-up 1988-89
Zenith Data Systems Cup runner-up 1990-91
Wales caps: 58

'He had a rapid rise to stardom and remained an Evertonian to his core'

JOE Royle was an Everton Giant, physically as well as statisically.

When he made his senior debut at the astonishingly young age of 16 years 282 days, he was already a strapping six footer with a broad, robust frame.

He actually played his junior football at right-half, but he was always destined to become one of the club's legendary No. 9s and made his debut at centre-forward in place of crowd idol Alex Young in 1966.

That baptism of fire at Blackpool ensured Royle became the youngest debutant in the club's history – and even though James Vaughan was 11 days younger when he stepped off the substitutes' bench to score against Crystal Palace in 2005, Royle is still rightly proud that no other Evertonian has started a senior match at a younger age.

One of the handful of Blues' strikers to score a century of league goals, he enjoyed a rapid rise to stardom, utilising his imposing physique to good effect as he fired his way into the First Division scoring charts.

In four seasons between 1967 and 1971, he rifled a remarkable 95 goals from 158 League and Cup appearances.

His power and goals made him a crucial member of the 1970 Championship-winning side when he top-scored with 23 league goals.

He struck another 23 goals in all competitions the following season – an unsuccessful one for the club by the standards set in previous campaigns – before a niggling back injury began to afflict him more and more.

Other marksmen were enlisted as he struggled to recover from a number of operations, and he was only 25 when he exited Everton for Manchester City.

But he remained an Evertonian to his core and a return was always inevitable.

He scored his final goal in football at Goodison Park, for Norwich City, eliciting affectionate cheers from the home fans who remembered him fondly.

He ignited those fires again in the winter of 1994 when he replaced Mike Walker as manager.

He rescued Everton from a seemingly hopeless position at the bottom of the Premier League table, beating

Millennium Giant   2004

Liverpool in his first match.

In fact, throughout his managerial spell at Everton he remained unbeaten by the Reds.

Just six months after arriving he guided the Blues to FA Cup glory at Wembley against Manchester United – still the last major silverware lifted by the Blues, and the last major trophy claimed by an English-born manager!

He guided the club to sixth in 1996, but a succession of injuries and a short-term dip in results led to his departure in 1997.

But he remained a true Blue and can be regularly spotted at Goodison Park to this day, watching intently from the Main Stand as the modern Blues seek to match his illustrious exploits.

JOE ROYLE FACTFILE

Born: Liverpool, 1949
Everton Appearances: 276
Everton Goals: 119
Everton Honours (player): First Division
Championship winner 1969-70
FA Cup runner-up 1968
FA Charity Shield winner 1970
Everton Manager: 1994-1997
Everton Honours (manager): FA Cup winner 1995
FA Charity Shield winner 1995
England caps: 6

'With 159 goals in 447 appearances, Sharp is second only to the immortal Dixie'

IT is an accepted fact of Everton life that Dixie Dean's remarkable goalscoring record will stand for all time.

A tally of 383 goals in 433 appearances is simply unattainable in the modern game, even by the most prolific of marksmen.

But with 159 goals in his 446 appearances, Graeme Sharp is second only to the immortal Dixie in the annals of Everton marksmen.

And his list of honours achieved at the club is second to none.

He was voted onto the list of Everton Giants in 2005, exactly 20 years after he top-scored during the most successful season in the club's long history.

But when he arrived at Goodison in April 1980 from Dumbarton, it was as a relative unknown.

He didn't take long to make Evertonians start to sit up and take notice.

A stunning televised strike against Tottenham Hotspur in January 1982 caused a stir and was voted ITV's Goal of the Month.

And when fellow Scot Andy Gray arrived at the club in November 1983, the pair began to forge a close liaison on and off the field.

Pals off the pitch, feared strike partners on it, the original "Bruise Brothers" terrorised defences - especially on the big occasion.

Sharp's volley which secured a first victory at Anfield for 14 years in 1984 is rated by many Evertonians as the greatest Everton goal of all-time.

He also opened the scoring in the 1984 FA Cup final, and the following season put his name on the scoresheet 30 times in 54 games.

But strangely it wasn't as an out-and-out goalscorer that Sharp's reputation was built.

He was recognised more as an unselfish provider for others - so much so that when Ian Rush endured his ill-fated stint at Juventus in the 1987-88 season, he was asked who he would prefer as a strike partner.

With the cream of the world's strikers to choose from, Rush chose Sharp.

Happily Sharp's departure from Everton was non-negotiable and he made almost 450 appearances in

Millennium Giant   2005

Royal Blue, continuing to score goals throughout his career and acting as a nursemaid to a succession of strikers ranging from Gary Lineker to Tony Cottee.

His list of honours at Everton spoke volumes.

So, too, did his longevity as a front-line forward at Goodison Park.

When it was finally announced he was leaving Everton in the summer of 1991, to Joe Royle's Oldham Athletic for £500,000, he was 30-years-old and his goals tally had begun to diminish.

But there were many Evertonians who still believed he had been released too soon.

Following the "Once a Blue, Always a Blue" motto to the letter, he returned to the club as a fans' liaison officer, where he has continued to devote loyal service to the Royal Blue cause.

GRAEME SHARP FACTFILE

Born: Glasgow, 1960
Everton Appearances: 446
Everton Goals: 159
Everton Honours: First Division Championship winner 1984-85, 1986-87, runner-up 1985-86
FA Cup winner 1984, runner-up 1985, 1986, 1989
European Cup Winners' Cup winner 1984-85
League Cup runner-up 1983-84
FA Charity Shield winner 1984, 1985, 1986 (shared), 1987
Simod Cup runner-up 1988-89
Scotland caps: 12

'His outstanding technique, vision and ability was instrumental in a Royal Blue revival'

HE was the rottweiler with the best of breed pedigree, the bristling midfield terrier who combined class and vision.

But while it's impossible to even contemplate the suggestion now, when Howard Kendall signed a then 26-year-old Peter Reid from Bolton Wanderers for £60,000 in December 1982, he was considered damaged goods and a gamble.

Reid's ability as a player had never been questioned – indeed Gordon Lee had bid £600,000 to try and secure his services several years earlier – but since those days, Reid had suffered a series of career-threatening injuries.

He suffered two broken legs, torn knee ligaments – ironically in a snow-covered match against Everton which was subsequently abandoned – then a cartilage operation.

It took him 12 months to rediscover his form and fitness and force his way into Howard Kendall's starting line-up, but when he did he became the heartbeat of an irresistible Royal Blue revival.

A fierce and uncompromising competitor, his never-say-die attitude blended superbly with other infectious characters like Andy Gray, Kevin Ratcliffe and Graeme Sharp.

But his outstanding technique, vision and ability to deliver a penetrating through ball was instrumental in helping Everton to the most successful period in the club's history.

His engine was superb and it was no coincidence that the most injury-free season of his entire career should also coincide with the most successful in Everton's long history.

Reid was voted PFA Player of the Year in 1985, after inspiring Everton to the brink of an unprecedented treble.

Two years later, despite suffering ankle problems which limited him to 11 league outings, it was his return to the starting line-up which proved the telling factor in Everton's second league title success in three years.

It was a glorious era in the club's history. And Reid's significance was underlined by skipper Kevin Ratcliffe. On the night Reid was welcomed onto the list of Everton Giants, he said: "He was a winner, a leader and a dream

Millennium Giant 2006

to play alongside. He made everything look easy, he kept it simple and he made sure other players could play."

A boyhood Liverpool fan, Reid now proudly proclaims himself as an Evertonian.

When receiving his Everton Giant accolade, he said: "To have been able to play for this club is fantastic. To be described as a legend is beyond my wildest dreams.

"I lost my dad earlier this year. He, like me, was born a Red but converted to an Evertonian.

"My mum was the one with the brains in the family because she has always been a Blue. This award will take pride of place at my mum's house and every time I look at it I will think of my old fella."

When he retired from playing in 1994, he had accumulated 642 senior appearances and 41 goals. He earned 13 England caps as a player and went on to enjoy a successful spell in charge of Sunderland between 1995 and 2002, leading the Black Cats to Championship glory in 1999.

He also managed Manchester City with some distinction and played for Queens Park Rangers, but it was in the Royal Blue of Everton that he enjoyed his finest hours.

PETER REID FACTFILE

Born: Liverpool, 1956
Everton Appearances: 234
Everton Goals: 13
Everton Honours: First Division Championship winner 1984-85, 1986-87, runner-up 1985-86
FA Cup winner 1984, runner-up 1985, 1986
European Cup Winners' Cup winner 1984-85
League Cup runner-up 1983-84
FA Charity Shield winner 1984, 1985, 1987
PFA Player of the Year 1984-85
England caps: 13

'"£70,000 is an insult to Colin Harvey, the White Pele" declared a banner ...'

WHEN Colin Harvey ended a 14-year association with Everton in September 1974, Sheffield Wednesday rubbed their hands in glee at having picked up a bargain.

Evertonians, however, were less thrilled.

'£70,000 is an insult to Colin Harvey, the White Pele,' declared a banner draped over the enclosure wall at the next home game.

If the transfer fee hadn't been hatched as an insult to Harvey, the banner at least underlined the depth of affection the player was held in by the fans.

Some Evertonians' achievements are registered in the number of great games they have produced for the club.

It would be more accurate to measure Harvey's greatness in the number of years' sterling service he gave to the club.

It was only a matter of time before he was voted onto the Giants' roster, and when he was it could have been for his achievements both on or off the park.

On it, Harvey made his Everton debut at the tender age of 18 - on the most daunting stage imaginable.

He made his bow in a European Cup tie in the San Siro Stadium against then European giants Inter Milan.

Fireworks, smoke bombs and the baying of 90,000 excitable Italian fans failed to intimidate a raw, but assured youngster.

After such a rarified introduction to senior football, he then returned to the more mundane surroundings of the Central League and reserve-team football to finish his education.

But within months he was back in a first-team jersey, this time for good.

Harvey possessed every attribute of a modern midfielder. He was quick, sharp in the tackle, possessed awesome stamina, had vision, superb close control and the ability to deliver a telling pass.

Perhaps the only facet missing from his armoury was a regular goals contribution, but the ones he did supply were usually memorable - like the winner in the 1966 FA Cup semi-final against Manchester United, or the piledriving 25-yard screamer which clinched the 1969-70 League Championship against West Bromwich Albion.

When he received his Giants award from Kevin

Millennium Giant   2007

Ratcliffe, he declared: "This is a great honour. I have been privileged to play for this club."

But it wasn't just as a player that Harvey devoted venerable service to the Blues.

He returned as a youth-team coach and many judges believe it was his promotion from duty with the youngsters to first-team coaching alongside Howard Kendall and Mick Heaton that was the catalyst to greatness in the 1980s.

He became a reluctant manager of the club when Howard Kendall moved to Spain in 1987, and while his achievements suffered in comparison to what had gone before, in hindsight his record was better than many believed.

He took Everton to FA Cup and Simod Cup finals in 1989, a Littlewoods Cup semi-final and finished fourth, eighth and sixth in successive seasons.

But he was always more comfortable directing operations behind the scenes, and he was delighted to step back into coaching when Howard Kendall returned to the club for his second spell in charge in 1990.

Harvey was altogether happier back in charge of the youngsters though, and he was responsible for the club winning the FA Youth Cup again in 1998, reaching the final in 2002 - and overseeing the production of talent which included Wayne Rooney.

When he finally announced his retirement from the club in 2003, he had devoted more than 40 years' service to Everton Football Club.

A man of the people, indeed.

COLIN HARVEY FACTFILE

Born: Liverpool, 1944
Everton Appearances: 387
Everton Goals: 24
Everton Honours (player): First Division Championship winner 1969-70
FA Cup winner 1966, runner-up 1968
FA Charity Shield winner 1970
Everton Manager: 1987-1990
Everton Honours (manager): FA Cup runner-up 1989
FA Charity Shield winner 1987
Simod Cup runner-up 1988-89
England caps: 1

POSTSCRIPT

Hollywood to Goodison:
With legendary actor
Sylvester Stallone during
his visit in 2007

'I've always referred to Everton as one big, extended family – my family. The People's Club seems to embrace that whole idea'

I ALWAYS thought that Thursday March 14th, 2002, might be an important day in Everton's history. I'd been talking to a nearby club for 24 hours about the acquisition of their manager.

I felt he had the qualities to take Everton back to where we belonged.

It was around 6.30pm on that evening that I rang David from a hotel room in Haydock and said: "The good news is that you are the new manager of Everton. The bad news is that you've got a press reception in an hour's time at Goodison Park!"

David jumped in his car and he and I had time only to give each other a resolute handshake before he walked into a large room, sat down at a long table, and met the nation's press!

It was within minutes of that entrance that I can remember thinking to myself: "This man is good ... he knows exactly how to conduct himself and handle the media."

And seconds later I realised how good he was! He came out with five words that were destined to go into the folklore of our beloved football club.

"Everton are the People's Club."

FINAL WORD

By Everton
chairman Bill
Kenwright

Everton

'Like Evertonians everywhere, I was gripped by the simplicity of the People's Club statement – and it underlined David's ability to do and say the right thing at the right time'

It was brilliant. A resonant, colourful and enduring catchphrase. And one that every Evertonian could relate to!

I've always referred to Everton as one big, extended family - my family. And the words "The People's Club" seems to embrace that whole idea.

Although I have lived and worked in London for over 40 years the only time I ever feel 'home' is when I arrive back on Merseyside. Back with my family - and my extended Everton family. But everywhere I go in the world there are reminders of that family.

I have been in the back of a car at a New York intersection when a man has peered in and shouted in an accent more Birkenhead than Brooklyn 'Alright Blue!'

I have been all over Europe and had people walk up to me and ask which players would be fit for the weekend!

I have seen iconic images of little boys in war-torn Iraq holding newspapers with Everton headlines - and like millions of others I have shared in the sorrows and tragedies that have befallen those who have either literally or figuratively worn our Blue jersey.

I've often said that the love affair with my football club has brought me more joy and pain than anything else in my life.

Every Evertonian will understand me when I say, you very seldom meet an Everton fan, you meet an Everton fanatic. We love our club with a passion that endures all the trials and tribulations that football, and indeed life, throws at us.

For that passion I have such a lot of people to be thankful to - from my all time idol, Dave Hickson, through Roy Vernon, Bobby Collins, Alex Young, Bally, Howard, Colin - Joe, Sharpy. The list could, and would, go on and on.

And of course I now add to that list David Moyes.

I have been blessed in my short time as Chairman in working with two exceptional men as the club's managers.

Walter Smith brought a stability and a dignity to our club at a time when we severely needed it.

The warmth with which he is always welcomed back by our fans is a testament to his credentials both as a man and manager.

David Moyes has been more than just a manager. He has been a real force of positivity, an inspiration, and, yes, a visionary ...

And that became patently apparent in the Captain's Table lounge on that fateful evening in March.

"This is The People's Club of Merseyside".

It was appropriate then, and it's still appropriate now. As far as I am concerned Everton is the greatest family in football.

I'm proud to be a member of that family.

Yes we are The People's Club.

Thank you David.

OTHER TITLES PRODUCED BY SPORT MEDIA:

'Everton's FA Cup
100'

'Everton Strange
But Blue'

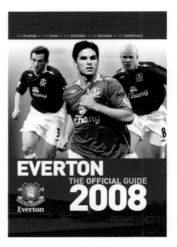

'Everton The Official
Guide 2008'

All of these titles are available to order online at www.merseyshop.com, by calling
0845 143 0001 or by sending a cheque payable to Sport Media at the following address:
Sport Media Books, PO Box 48, Old Hall Street, Liverpool, L69 3EB